Thundering Sneakers

Thundering Sneakers

by

Prudence Mackintosh

1981
Doubleday & Company, Inc.
Garden City, New York

Many of these chapters have appeared, in slightly different form, in *Texas Monthly*.

A *Christmas Diary* originally appeared as *Merry Christmas in Your House; Merry Chaos in Mine* in *Redbook Magazine*. Copyright © 1977 by the Redbook Publishing Company.

Library of Congress Cataloging in Publication Data Mackintosh, Prudence. Thundering sneakers. 1. Family—United States—Anecdotes, facetiae, etc. 2. Parent and child—United States—Anecdotes, facetiae, etc. I. Title. HQ536.M25 306.8′7
ISBN: 0-385-12879-7
Library of Congress Catalog Card Number: 80–1124

For John, Jack, Drew and William,
of course, but also for Anne Barnstone
and Bill Broyles.

Contents

Preface

THE FAMILY I began writing about six years ago has changed. We live in a different house, have an additional child, and, of course, we're older. Drew, my middle son, who once believed that a toothbrush kept under his pillow might make his teeth fall out for profit, is at last without his front teeth and complaining that the tooth fairy needs a briefing on inflation. Jack, the oldest son, is ten and has still not forgiven me for allowing him to miss the Soyuz-Apollo television coverage when he was five. "I'm just so embarrassed that it happened in my lifetime, and I didn't even know about it," he says. William, the baby who kept me out of step with my contemporaries by being born about the time everyone else was returning to law school, reassessing their marital status, or at least defining their "passages," is now three years old. A proud father who has a two-year-old son asked me recently if William knows his ABCs and numbers yet. "I haven't asked him," I replied. I hated to admit to the proud father that this third time around, the only preschool achievement short of a Mozart minuet that impresses me is toilet performance.

Three little boys have changed us. John, my husband, was a little disgruntled to see that the hunting license I purchased for him this year records his hair as gray. And at a luncheon recently with some (this dates me) girl friends, I grimaced to hear someone remark, "You know, I think we're all remarkably well preserved for middle age."

Middle-aged or not, we have mellowed and learned well the lesson our progeny forced on us—that life, at least life with children, must be appreciated in the process. Nothing much gets finished around here anymore. Writing about the process probably gave these years more form and order for me than they might have had otherwise. However, these chapters, many of which appeared first in *Texas Monthly*, never attempted to offer final solutions or pediatric advice—only the solace of shared experience. Perhaps they also offer an affirmation that our children's early years were not just an interruption in a writing career or in a good night's sleep, or a blur of mindless, boring tasks. To the contrary, they contained all of the loveliness, violence, humor, and mystery that we could handle.

Every anecdote recorded actually happened. I once met a very prolific woman writer who had just published a book of essays about family life. Having read on her book jacket that she had three children, I was, of course, eager to ask her how she found the time to write so much with three children around. "Well," she said sheepishly, "I really have only two; I made one of them up. I thought adding a girl would make it more interesting."

Part One

Crossing into Thirty

THE PEANUT-butter-and-jelly luncheons at my house are often accompanied by heated, irrational debates as to who is bigger, older, or faster. The dispute usually begins with our two-year-old, who rises in his chair, lowers his voice two octaves, and announces, "I'm big." With partially chewed bite still apparent as he speaks, the four-year-old picks up the gauntlet with "I'm bigger, and I'm older than you—I'm four."

The two-year-old, depending on how eager he is to return to his sandwich, will either persist absurdly with "I'm bigger!" or acquiesce reluctantly with "Okay, shut up, you dumb bozo."

In late September, shortly after my birthday, I quashed one such debate and put the pecking order in its proper perspective. "I'm thirty," I announced before the two-year-old could rise, "and I may not be the fastest anymore, but I'm still bigger than the two of you put together, so sit down and finish your lunch."

Thirty. It's a crisis time, according to the recent covers of at least two magazines. Divorce is rampant now among my contemporaries, and many of the marriages that remain intact are undergoing serious review. I've been spared that crisis. My husband's domestic talents predate any women's liberation requirements, and the only time I can recall that we had to "work" at our marriage was during a brief period before I agreed to discard a superfluous suitcase full of shoes as we trekked across Europe on our honeymoon.

Thirty. There is a nagging suspicion that I am not really as "big" as I am supposed to be. In times of real emergency, such as the partial severing of a two-year-old's finger by a slammed door, or on viewing a hammer-gashed forehead, I still look around for the "real" mother to take charge. Surely I cannot be old enough to bear the responsibility.

However, I have begun to note telltale signs of age. Physical signs among my female contemporaries are minimal—a thinning of the face and thickening of the thigh perhaps, but on the whole, they look younger and better than they did in our high school days. We are the high school class of '62, whose yearbook photographs with tight permanent waves and red lipstick look eighteen going on forty-five. So now, it isn't *our* appearance so much as it is the fact that policemen have begun to look too young to be of much assistance these days. Young men and women interviewing at my husband's law firm are cautiously beginning to put a "Mr." before his name, and quite frankly I'm beginning to yawn when they ask the same idealistic questions that I asked six years ago. "How much time does the firm allot to *pro bono* work?"

The clincher occurred last spring. My husband and I ventured onto the campus of Southern Methodist University, near our home in Dallas, to see an old friend's award-winning film, *Badlands*, at the USA Film Festival. After the showing, our film-maker friend was swamped by auto-

It never occurred to me to make anything up—especially my third male child. The real material at hand always came faster and fresher than any I could have created.

graph seekers and aspiring student film makers. Standing to one side of the celebrity with a look that said, "I knew him when . . . ," I was approached by one young film student who asked, "Do you happen to know how old Mr. Malick is?"

"Yes," I smugly replied, "he's only thirty."

"Thank God," the obviously relieved freshman responded, "that means I've got at least twelve years to make it big."

Stunned, I came home and tried desperately to recall what, as an eighteen-year-old, I thought I would have accomplished by my thirtieth birthday. At eighteen my roommates and I were performing some sort of balancing act that included the mysteries of University of Texas sorority life, a fairly heavy academic load, the slightly suspect university Y.M.C.A., and an unwashed serape-clad beatnik such as Dave, who saw it as his mission in life to save us from ourselves and our misguided cultural legacy. Knowing full well that we were pledged to seek "the good, the true, and the beautiful" at chapter meetings in secret basement rooms of the sorority house every Monday night, Dave delighted in showing up at our posh dormitory on his bicycle (a most unacceptable mode of transportation in those days) to offer us a ride to a Scientology lecture. The summer after our freshman year, he sent us each postcards exhorting, "You are better than animals. Do not be satisfied with 'birth, reproduction, diversion, and death.'" An appropriately heavy reading list followed, to which we responded with a postcard bearing small paw prints.

But we were serious students, even if our grade point averages occasionally belied the fact. We flaunted illegally obtained "stack passes" that enabled us to go into the musty carrels of the library reserved for graduate students, and we flocked to see Ingmar Bergman movies at the Student Union.

Women's liberation had not yet dawned, and we somehow saw no incongruity in running from a philosophy seminar on the nature of prejudice to a "Ten Most Beautiful" interview. Our most radical political involvement had to do with the National Students' Association, and though we sat through heated debates and handed out leaflets, I can't even remember whether we were for it or against it. We lamely protested our fathers' demands that we take the "female insurance policy"—twelve hours of education courses—but our career goals were poorly defined, and no one pressed us to define them. Summers spent working in Washington in glorified secretarial positions called "summer internships" may have made us briefly consider life as the wife of an aspiring politician, but we did not seriously contemplate political careers for ourselves.

If we were ill suited for moneymaking careers, we were even less prepared for life as wife and mother. We smugly believed that anyone who could read could cook; our husbands have not forgotten the early days of ground meat in gray sauce that resulted. Never in my wildest dreams at eighteen would I have predicted that my age thirty accomplishments would include beef Wellington or a loaf of homemade French bread.

We are thirty now. Oh, Dirty Dave, where are you? I won't fault you if you're a sales representative for IBM. Although I reread Sterne's *Tristram Shandy* last year as Professor Eliosef said we should at twenty-nine, I'm a bit fuzzy on "appearance versus reality" and quite frankly the "objective correlative" has escaped me. I am not fluent in Spanish or French, and Book I of Bach's Preludes and Fugues collects dust on the piano. The summer of '66 that my husband and I spent in Europe will just have to do us for a while. We have two sons instead.

Our childless friends have been spear carriers in the opera, have traveled through the South of France, or basked on the beaches of Dubrovnik more than once. They take impulse trips to Zihuatenejo. Their coffee tables are unmolested, and we are glad that we know them. It is soothing occasionally to dine at a candlelit table where there is no fear of two small streakers bounding through yelling, "Get me. . . ."

But we do not envy their passing thirty and pondering, "Shall we have children or not?" In our twenties we pondered very little. We made art purchases impetuously, acquired an electric typewriter and a stereo, all of which we now know we couldn't possibly have afforded then. Had we waited until thirty to make a decision about having children, I'm quite sure we would now debate it through menopause. We're glad we didn't wait.

The raising of children, at least our children, is not always a rational process. There are days when we are Spock, Ginott, Piaget, and Montessori all rolled into one, and on those days we have no doubts that our children will rise up and call us blessed. Just as frequently, however, it is simply a matter of coping. Only this week I have blotted bloody heads twice. My four-year-old is so inured to the sight of his brother's blood that he often waits until I'm off the telephone to announce casually, "Mom, Drew's blooding again. He said he wanted my hammer, so I gave it to him." I have also been thrown out of my favorite branch of the public library because my two-year-old insisted on shouting "Burger King" while his brother did body rolls the length of the main desk. Later the same day at the post office the two-year-old took a bite out of the damp sponge in a dish on the table because big brother said it was cake. And only a day later I was seen behind an industrial-sized mop at Safeway mopping an easily identified amber puddle because the two-year-old couldn't wait until I finished writing my check.

My doctor, who once regarded me as relaxed, cool, and unflappable, now gazes out the window as I recite the symptoms of what seems to me to be advanced stomach paralysis. His eyes glaze slightly, and I know that he no longer sees me as he begins, "Young mothers often have these complaints. In these times of stress and strain, we must not be ashamed to admit the effects of tension. . . ."

The long bathtub "soaker," that last bastion of privacy that restores my physical and mental equanimity, has now been invaded by small boys who never knock and who will ax the door if it's locked. "Gee, Mom, I bet you were lonely in here all by yourself," they say. Leaning on the tub, they reject the "Mr. Rogers' Neighborhood" theory that "Everybody's fancy, everybody's fine. Your body's fancy and so is mine." By their standards I am funny, not "fancy."

Though I take pride in their occasional civility toward neighbors or grandparents, I cannot regard them as my age thirty accomplishments; they are not finished. In fact, nothing much gets finished around here anymore, and they have forced us to appreciate the processes of living rather than the finished results. Taking freshly baked bread from the oven is never quite as important anymore as deciding earlier who gets to "slug it when it gets all puffy."

Crayon on the dining room wall, Lincoln Logs in the instep, and perpetually spilled milk are small prices to pay for the dimensions they add to our lives. To open my sleep-encrusted eyes to a soft pat on the arm and a small voice that says, "I gwad see you soo much, Mama," is far better than the jolt of an electric alarm clock. Who but a two-year-old notices the faint moon in the midmorning sky, or looks at birds hopping around our bird feeder and says, "Dance, Mom?" And who but a four-year-old hyperventilates twice in one afternoon trying to learn to whistle?

The self-knowledge that my children continually force on me is occasionally painful, but far less expensive than group encounters and analysis. Recently in a rare idle moment, I polished my fingernails, something I'm sure I haven't done in at least five years. My older son was irate. "Mama," he yelled, "you'll have to get that stuff off right now."

"Why?" I asked, admiring the chic effect of Cool Copper. "Haven't you ever seen a lady with nail polish before?"

"Yeah, but you're the lady who's supposed to help us dig those holes this afternoon."

They catch every hint of hypocrisy. "How come Daddy bought a new rake instead of finding the old one behind that junk in the storeroom? You always say that we can't have new stuff just because we've lost the old stuff."

Their profane utterances mirror our own and cause our backs to stiffen. We're strong on "Aw, shucks" now.

Our children keep our egos remarkably trim. I am not much with a football, but on reaching my thirtieth birthday I do read stories with as many as three different voices, make up original lullabies, and bake creditable chocolate chip cookies. So what do they think I do best? "Wash dishes," the four-year-old replies without hesitation. I am not seriously wounded; he thinks his trial attorney father's forte is hedge clipping.

Their admiration is at times unbounded. Sitting on the floor of a clothing store dressing room with amazing patience, the four-year-old watches as I desperately exhaust the sale racks in search of a long skirt. "Oh, Mama, if you wear that one, you'll have to be a queen, but if you get the blue one, I think you'll be a beautiful dancer lady." To his three-foot stature, I am not a short and slightly dumpy five feet four inches. He empties his piggy bank and says, "When I get some more money, I'll buy you dresses like Cher wears."

At this point I have few rivals for their affection. Talk of growing up and marrying some girl (other than the thirteen-year-old baby sitter who runs me a close second) always ends with some Oedipal remark about their being already married to me.

And despite my thirtieth birthday, there is strong opposition to my aging. A serious autumn conversation about how we all grow older like the leaves on the trees ended abruptly with the stamping of a small foot and the shaking of a finger, "You will never, never, never be an old lady. Never!"

Like Erica in Alison Lurie's novel *The War Between the Tates,* I too may come to view them in years ahead as "awful lodgers who pay no rent, whose leases cannot be terminated." In the meantime, I'm playing a pretty fair Cat Woman to their Batman and Robin. And for a thirty-year-old with so little training, that's making it big.

Pacem in Terrors

LAST WEEK it occurred to Drew, my two-year-old, that his older brother does not have a divine right to the Zooper Looper that comes in the Cheerio box. And I think that means that things are going to get worse around here before they get better.

"Can't we just send him on back to heaven?" Jack, my four-year-old, asks in disgust as he watches his younger brother dutifully shovel in the last bite of spinach, a prerequisite for the meager dessert that will now have to be shared. "I'll bet Gene Blakeney would give me his brother."

My firstborn was a little more than two years old at Drew's birth. We did everything the books instructed to ease the jealousy. We read Ezra Jack Keats' *Peter's Chair*, a charmingly illustrated tale of a little boy who discovers that he really is too big for his baby bed and small chair and who finally agrees to help his father paint them pink for new baby sister Susie. We arranged for him to view the less than beautiful baby at the hospital, bought a toy helicopter for the baby to present to his big brother on arrival at home, and for at least the first three months of his life we virtually ignored the newborn whenever big brother was present. Jack rewarded our efforts by demonstrating the inadequacies of his toilet training on the front sidewalk in the presence of five finicky neighbors.

My well-meaning pediatrician assured me that in three months my older boy would have no recollection of life without a brother. I took little comfort from that. Would he also have no recollection of what I regard as the halcyon days of my motherhood? Those were the days when he lolled in his playpen while I wrote piano melodies for Mother Goose rhymes about boys named Jack. Those were also the days when we made unnecessary trips to the grocery store just to collect smiles from sweet old ladies.

There are few smiles for us at Safeway now. The stock boy, who remembers that my kid is the one who pops wheelies with the grocery cart, stands guard over his precariously stacked cans of V-8. Halfway through the shopping list, I encounter innocent, fashionably dressed women and their pink, powdered first babies cooing over the Gerber's counter and wonder if they will fall from grace as I have. I feebly apologize when they find it necessary to lift their carts over my four-year-old, who has prostrated himself in the aisle in front of Captain Crunch with hopes of wearing down my nutritional scruples. Drew, who under duress still rides in the kiddie seat of the grocery cart, smiles coyly at sweet little ladies and then, well tutored by his older brother, yells "Karate chop" when they try to chuck him under the chin. At the counter, I look up from my check writing to see that Jack is climbing on top of the gum machine. "You'll fall," I say. "But I won't hurt myself," he replies, and he's right. He falls squarely on his soft brother, whose head it is that bangs into the grocery carts. Two children at the grocery store at 4 P.M. bring me to the realization that one child was none.

With a second son in tow, I am no longer the consistent, reasonable parent I intended to be. I shamelessly resort to bribery and/or spanking for expedience and am occasionally guilty of allowing my children to overdose themselves on wretched TV cartoons. Earlier this week when they appeared barefoot for the fourth time in one cold day, I bounced their sneakers off the wall in uncontrolled rage. (I concur with a friend who says children should have their feet laminated until they are able to tie their own shoelaces.) My dentist says I'll need orthodontic treatment if I don't quit gritting my teeth.

Before my second son was born, a mother of two confessed to me that she had spent the better part of a day setting the kitchen timer to buzz at ten-minute intervals to enforce the peaceful sharing of a rusty cap pistol found in the alley by her two boys. I distinctly remember murmuring, "Ridiculous." I now beg her forgiveness. I have gone to more absurd extremes to avoid confrontations, particularly before I've had my first cup of coffee in the morning. The sibling bickering can be set off by my carelessly dispensing different-colored chewable vitamins. "I wanted the orange one. You always give him the orange one." I have learned to ask, "Would someone please go get the newspaper?" only if one child is still asleep, or if it is Monday or Thursday, when the milk cartons on the porch provide an equally important alternate chore. One slip-up on my part and the morning paper is shredded in the living room by two small helpers screaming, "She said for me to bring it!" "No, my turn!" If one of them perchance gets it to the table intact, it is often necessary to return it to the porch so that the other one can provide equal service.

Variations on the same rivalrous theme occur throughout the day. "He flushed my potty," the two-year-old shrieks. Or at lunchtime, Jack can always draw Drew off side with the primeval taunt, "Nyah, nyah, nyah, nyah, nyah, I got the blue cup." If I hand him the red cup, it's the same tune, different color. The two-year-old responds by throwing his milk or spitting—crimes punishable by spanking at our house.

It is easy to fault the older child. He is more articulate, an adept con man, and he knows precisely which taunts will strike a responsive chord. He knows how to intone a question like, "Want me to rip your arm off?" so that his brother will say, "Yes." He has traded his brother more apple slices for cookies than I care to remember. He creates clever games where he is the jumper and his brother is always the hurdle. He deliberately trips over his little brother's feet as a pretext for vengeance.

However, I have observed these boys long enough to know that the younger child is not guiltless. If Jack fails to provoke a battle, I have seen Drew climb out of his high chair, pull up his shirt, and say, "You can't get my tummy." This may elicit one or two playful pokes from his brother. However, if the two-year-old is foolish enough to run in for a third poke, he always gets a gut-wrencher. The villain has full protection. "He told me to do it, Mom."

Drs. Benjamin Spock, Haim Ginott, Fitzhugh Dodson, and William E. Homan assure me that the scene is normal. Though Spock may be anathema in many homes, I still find solace in my battered volume. (It always flops open to those dog-eared pages which we read so frequently and nervously as novice parents: Infant bowel movements, varieties of.) Spock advised parents in his 1945 volume *The Common Sense Book of Baby and Child Care* to prepare the older child for the arrival of a sibling, to treat each child as an individual, to avoid comparison among siblings, to accept and mirror children's feelings, and to generally keep out of their fights. All of this advice is echoed in more recent popular volumes by pediatricians less tainted by politics.

I rather like Dr. William E. Homan (*Child Sense: A Pediatrician's Guide for Today's Families*) because he explodes the theory held by the others that it helps to prepare a child for the birth of a sibling. He and Dr. Fitzhugh Dodson (*How to Parent* and *How to Father*) use a similar analogy to help parents appreciate the first child's position when the second child arrives. Dodson writes in *How to Parent*: "Suppose that tomorrow your husband informs you of the following delightful bit of news. 'Dear,' he says, 'next week Roxanne my old girl friend will be joining us. Of course, I love you as much as I always have. And I will be with you on Mondays, Wednesdays, and Fridays. But on Tuesdays, Thursdays, and Saturdays, I will be with her. Sundays we will put up for grabs.' Furthermore, when this rival actually comes to take up residence in your house, you discover that she does not intend to lift a finger to help you around the house. All she does is loll around all day, reading women's magazines and drinking milk punches. How would you feel about Roxanne?"

But Dr. Homan takes the analogy a step further by asking, "Would it help much if your husband told you far in advance about his plans to bring the old girl home?" And to mothers who say, "Surely my twelve-year-old won't be jealous," Homan responds, "Of course not. You wouldn't mind if the second woman your husband chose were twelve years younger than you, would you?"

Dr. Haim Ginott has been so overused, or perhaps misunderstood, by my contemporaries that I sometimes think I will defy all he stands for and slug the next mother who says, "Do it with words, Jeremy," to the kid who just bloodied my kid's nose. Ginott's suggestions on nonviolence make good reading, but they require a verbal sophistication that just isn't practical for a four-year-old. For that matter, my two-year-old's verbal ability has grown phenomenally because of his brother's primitive teaching technique. "If you call this hammer a wrench one more time, I'll crush your head with it."

A skeptical friend warns me that I should use Ginott's "draw-me-a-picture-to-show-me-how-you-feel-about-your-brother" method only if I really want to know. Her own five-year-old's drawing made a medieval torture chamber look like a health spa. Frankly, the expression of feelings gets so free at my house that I'd like to see a little repression.

Six years' age difference between my brother and me did little to diminish the tormenting and the bickering. It only increased my disadvantage. The power an older child holds over a younger sibling is irresistible. Because I was so much younger and a girl (those were the days when boys were admonished, "We don't hit little girls"), the physical abuse was minimal. However, there was the match incident when I was five. We were planning an unauthorized wiener roast in the backyard. "Here, Prudence," my brother said, handing me a lighted match, "don't let this go out whatever you do. We need it to light the fire. I've got to go in the house to get the mustard." I dutifully took it, delighted to be trusted with such responsibility. "Turn it upside down," he yelled from the back door, "it won't burn so fast." I did, and the tears spilled down my cheeks not so much from the pain of my smoldering finger, but because I had let the match go out. He berated me accordingly, and, thanks to his eleven-year-old friends who gleefully witnessed the incident, the story followed me well into adolescence.

Though I could not appreciate it at the time, his tormenting was remarkably creative. He once offered to fix lunch for a little friend and me. "Deviled ham sandwiches and Seven-Up, coming up," he said, cheerily spreading Dash dog food on slices of bread and dropping Alka-Seltzer tablets in the glasses. He still recalls how the reticent little friend politely cleaned her plate.

I worshiped him—even when he called my eleven-year-old boy friend with the aerodynamically protruding ears "the Trans Eddie." He never fought a battle for me, but his very existence allowed me to say, "I'll tell my big brother on you." Though I can't explain it, I understand my two-year-old's need for a gut-wrencher from his brother. "Why don't you just stay away from him?" I hear myself echoing my own mother's words. But, of course, I remember that being separated from my brother was the greatest punishment.

As this brother entered the rock perils of adolescence, I lost my role as "tattle tail" and became his staunchest defender. I was privy to all of his misdoings and was paid handsomely not to tell. The payoff wasn't nearly so important in cementing our closeness as the opportunity he offered me to be ten and a half going on sixteen. I knew his high school teachers by such irreverent, but appropriate, nicknames as Duckie, Mousie, or just Old Lady Walters. I sat patiently through poker games and on one occasion was served a beer at a local drive-in notorious for poor enforcement of the liquor laws. Like the childhood tormenting, his teen-age rebellion was creative. I shudder to recall that he once fed laxatives to a goat and turned it loose in the high school over the weekend. Perhaps I played Little Missionary to his Prodigal Son simply because I knew I could never flout authority with such style.

My husband was an only child. His childhood storybooks have been saved for my sons. They bear no tug-of-war scars. An enormous bag of marbles—steelies, clearies, cat's-eyes, aggies, etc., found by our sons in their grandmother's closet—reveals that their father was of the "greedy marbler" species, who had no brother to drop his hoarded treasures in the floor furnace. No wonder he finds what we now call the Cain and Abel Show at our house so unsettling.

The fact is, however, the rivalry has its redeeming features. In the midst of tension, tears, and raw nerves, we can also see glimmerings of affection, filial camaraderie, self-awareness, and even maturity.

Strange as it seems, it is this little brother who intervenes when the older son and I butt heads. "Make Mama happy? Give a kiss?" he says, melting the resolve I had mustered to spank.

Little brother, himself the worldly-wise second born with whom I have special rapport, cannot know what he missed or perhaps what he has been spared by getting a "used" mother. In a year or so we will read *I'll Fix Anthony* by Judith Viorst, a little brother's superb lament and fantasy about what he will do to his big brother when he is six. (For little girls with older brothers, I recommend Charlotte Zolotow's *Big Brother*, or for bossy big sisters, *Big Sister and Little Sister* by the same author.) My baby boy's position as second son allows him to be two going on four. Because his brother told him he looked like a girl in the beautiful hand-me-down Lord Fauntleroy suits, he has worn blue jeans that hang low on his hips since he was eighteen months old. He was a twenty-two-month-old toilet prodigy, thanks to his brother's example. His first sentence was predictably, "Give a turn." The treasures I find in his pockets tell me that he has occasionally been permitted to dig with his brother's pirate gang in the forbidden alley. Only a second-born two-year-old goes around singing, "Popeye the sailor man, he lives in a garbage can." Though he is battered daily, he wakes from his nap—just as I did years ago—saying, "Where's my brother?"

How has a younger brother enhanced my older son's life? If I ask him what he thinks of his brother, I am likely to get a cryptic reply like, "Did you know that he eats the muscles out of his dolls?" We read Charlotte Zolotow's *If It Weren't for You*, a big brother's fantasy of what life would be like without a little brother. The older brother notes that the last slice of cake would always be his, and no one would ever say, "Set an example." He concludes, however, "I'd have to be alone with those grown-ups."

Without the second child, I might not have seen the beginning of a conscience so early in the first one. Contrition is not one of his strong points, but I have seen him cry when he has committed a deliberate act of violence such as shoving his brother, tricycle and all, head first into the street. "Are you crying because you know you'll be punished?" I ask. "No," he hiccups with sincere remorse, "he's my brother and I pushed him and a car could have hit him."

Occasionally when other children come to play, someone will accuse his little brother of foul play. I am amused to hear the four-year-old come to his sibling's defense: "He didn't kick you. He never kicks anyone unless I tell him to."

His nursery-school teacher complains to me that on Fridays my older son refuses to join the story circle. He sits with face pressed to the sliding glass door that looks out on a playground because he knows Friday's the day his little brother is at "baby school" and will appear on the playground. "Pssst, Drew," the older brother beckons with stage whispers until little Drew's nose is pressed against the glass door outside. "Don't come over here. You have to go play with your baby friends."

A giant helium-filled balloon that has given the two-year-old much pleasure gets popped as the two boys are dueling with my electric mixer beaters on a cold, rainy afternoon. I listen in amazement as my older son, instead of taunting, "Nyah, nyah, crybaby," imparts the verities of life to his wailing brother. "You know, Drew, every balloon has to pop. I never had one yet that didn't."

Tykes Bearing Gifts

IF YOU ever doubted original sin, or for a fleeting moment believed in the innate goodness of man, you missed my four-year-old's birthday party. Primal greed and innocent ingratitude were rampant. Presents were hoarded by the honoree. One package cleverly decorated with chewing gum was stripped by the donor before being relinquished. Combat-hardened veterans (six-year-olds) trooped in popping balloons and laying odds that they could see through the blindfold to pin the tail on the donkey or at least blow out all the candles on the cake before the honoree inhaled. I broke a pledge from my own childhood by muttering repeatedly, as each gift was opened, the time-worn birthday phrase, "What do you *say*, Jack?"

One father candidly confided before the party started, "Patrick really doesn't like to see another kid getting all that loot, so don't encourage him to watch the unwrapping."

The loot bothers me, too, for a different reason. The conflict between my compulsive parental overindulgence and what must be my legacy from the Great Depression always takes its toll at birthday time.

I never really knew the Depression, but I do know that

it is wicked to drink Welch's grape juice undiluted. I never cared much for oranges in my stocking Christmas morning either, but I'm outraged when my own son says, "Hey, who put this dummy orange in my stocking?" My children don't even believe the chicken wing is white meat.

A shamefaced friend admitted recently that her children had never really known the sweet agony of wanting something badly for a long period of time. "Have you noticed that kids ask each other, 'What are you *getting* for your birthday?' By age four they already know it's simply a matter of coordinating their requests with birthdays, Christmas, or perhaps Mom and Dad's guilt-ridden return from a vacation without them."

Would my children never know the "character-building" experience of wanting and being denied? My brother and I learned early that things excessively desired were routinely denied.

The Great Depression won out for the first few years of my four-year-old's life. For at least the first eighteen months he knew cucumber slices as "cookies." Cokes were unknown, and when he once mistakenly labeled the gum ball machine at the grocery store "vitamins," I never saw fit to correct him.

As for birthdays, the first one was celebrated with a cake, a birthday hat, and Mom and Dad. On his second birthday, his best friend joined us for a fifteen-minute adventure on a Dallas Transit bus from our house to the end of the line and back. Ice cream and cake on the porch afterward attracted a few other neighborhood children, who, realizing it was a birthday celebration, ran home and returned with "used" presents—a naked wigless baby doll, a puzzle with missing pieces, and a storybook—all somehow very nice because the gifts were unexpected and generously given.

At three years a favorite five-year-old from San Antonio joined him for a day at Six Flags Amusement Park with Daddy. Again presents were unanticipated, and there was something refreshingly innocent about his "For me?"

Though he attended dozens of "real" birthday parties during those three years, he never once expressed any desire to have a gala of his own. In retrospect, most parties prior to age four were less than joyous occasions. A standard two- or three-year-old's birthday party generally follows this scenario: tears and considerable physical struggle before we leave home because the party requires Sunday-school clothes. More tears on arrival at party when it becomes necessary to wrench the gift for the birthday child from son's hand. Performing magicians or clown-faced mothers cause toilet-training regression. The opening of presents disconcerts all guests and without one mother per child there is a good chance that all presents will be destroyed within moments after unwrapping. After the serving of the cake and ice cream, everything degenerates fast. Infant-seated younger babies, who have placidly watched the older children, now lose their pacifiers; children with huge clods of chocolate frosting stuck in their sneaker treads climb over the white velvet sofa, flash cubes fail, balloons pop, and the hostess discovers that she has only eight favors for nine children.

On the way home, older child gets a Tootsie Pop inextricably tangled in my hair and the baby throws up an entire box of raisins.

So why did we decide to go all out for this fourth birthday? There were several reasons. Perhaps we had some need to relive what we thought were the real pleasures of our own childhood. Or perhaps we never got that Schwinn bike we wanted and here's our chance. This particular party also grew out of Christmas guilt. With smug self-righteousness we instructed Santa to leave a red wagon for both boys instead of the much desired Big Wheel. (For those who never watched "Captain Kangaroo," a Big Wheel is a plastic red, blue, and yellow *Easy Rider* type of tricycle.) I objected to the Big Wheel for two reasons: (a) we already had a three-wheel riding toy—a tricycle, (b) it looks like a motorcycle. My sons are always in the market for a mom with higher regard for motorcycles and guns.

Jack's disappointment Christmas morning was not immediately evident. A red wagon is, after all, a pretty neat surprise until you open the front door and are confronted by six friends on shiny Big Wheels. The humiliation of peddling into this crowd on his old tricycle was probably the same humiliation my husband suffers each year after the firm's Christmas party when the parking attendant at the Dallas Country Club wheels up in our '65 Chevrolet.

So we made our atonement with the silent resolve that he would have a real party this year. Hang the Big Wheel, he'd be the first kid on the block with a real bicycle for his birthday in May.

The honoree anticipated the party for at least a month by threatening his friends, "You better give that to me or you won't get to come to my burfday." When I heard him tell a neighbor's daughter that no girls would be allowed at the party, I thought I had an easy out. "Moms are not girls," he coolly informed me.

There are many Supermoms (at least two on my street) who can throw a birthday party for twenty-seven kids without becoming a shrew or a martyr. I can't. Threatening with every dollop of batter flung into the pan that she would sever the next fist that landed in the frosting, Shrew-Mom made the birthday cupcakes for the nursery school celebration three days before the real birthday party. It was Martyr-Mom who made the invitations. "I've spent the entire afternoon drawing Pooh Bears and balloons just because I love you so much and want you to have a nice party. The least you could do is color them within the lines."

The party bore little resemblance to those of my childhood. Family albums recall fluffy, sashed Kate Greenaway dresses, white tableclothes, fluted nut cups, Bobo the Magician entertaining a roomful of awed children in the ceiling-fan-cooled Palm Room of the Grim Hotel. My son's party had only eight little boys in the backyard. Balloons briefly festooned the trees. Guests wisely wore blue jeans, and I don't recall anyone ever sitting down at the paper-covered picnic table. The games I'd planned to last an hour were exhausted in ten minutes. To compensate, I read a Winnie the Pooh story. To add a little drama to the reading, I popped a hidden balloon at a crucial moment. Jack, worn out from party anticipation, burst into tears. "You didn't tell me you were going to do that," he wailed.

On to more important things—the presents. They were bountiful, and no one said thank you for anything without being coerced. But that night before bedtime, as I watched the honoree lining up the shiny Tonka crane beside the butterfly net, and the Sesame Street book and the colors and the puzzle and the sand scoop, I realized something that the Supermoms probably knew a long time ago. Austerity is a quality for moms—not kids.

Rag Time

IT OCCURRED to me, while flipping through some second-hand copies of *Vogue* given to me by a friend who already seems to have her camel, gray, rust, and burgundy tones perfectly coordinated, that those arbiters of fashion, Grace Mirabella and Diana Vreeland, have about as much influence on my wardrobe as I have on my children's appearance.

My son Jack left for kindergarten this morning in a Snoopy sweatshirt that doesn't cover his belly button, a pair of Toughskin jeans that weren't tough enough, and sneakers that galloped in the dryer from six-thirty to seven-thirty this morning. It was cold, but he refused a sweater. Under protest he has worn three different wraps to school and conveniently left all of them in his locker. He says his new sweater is a Christmas sweater (Scandinavian design), and he will be happy to wear it December 25.

I've quit fighting the Snoopy shirt. It is so ragged that we used it as a paint rag when we painted the breakfast room last month. It was tearfully retrieved from the garbage can and now Jack sleeps with it under his pillow so I can't destroy it. I'm not averse to repairing the pocket

that hangs by two threads on the seat of his jeans. I'd
rather he'd put on one of his two other pairs of blue
jeans, which seem identical to me, but he refuses to wear
them because he says "they rattle." The gripper snaps at
the waist of these new jeans do make a little rattling
noise, but why would a child who speaks at least fifty
decibels louder than anyone I know even notice? He also
has two other pairs of sneakers. Why then do I rise at six-
thirty to start the dryer before I've even made the coffee?
Because this is one morning when I just don't feel like having a horrible, irrational confrontation. The scene usually
goes like this:

"Mom, I can't find my shoes."

"They're in your closet."

"No, not those, I mean my black-and-white ones."

"You stepped in a dog pie yesterday coming home from
school, remember? So you can wear the red-and-blue ones
today." I say in as innocuous a tone as I can muster.

"Oh, yeah," he nods sarcastically, "I guess you want me
to look like a girl. Those are girl shoes and you know it."

I butter the toast and try to take some comfort in the
fact that in some other household there is probably a
small daughter from my son's kindergarten class hurling a
red-and-blue sneaker at her mother and crying, "These
are boy shoes!"

"Well, what about the blue-and-white shoes with the
sprinter on the side? Those can't be girl shoes, can they?"

"Oh, gross, man." (My husband calls this Punky Public
School Talk and wants to know what I plan to do about
it.) "Those blue-and-white shoes have squishy insides."
(We paid extra for cushioned arch supports.) "I never do
touch the bases when I wear those, and the coach yells at
me."

The debate grows more irrational. His father puts

down the paper and offers the tired argument that there
are children in this world who have no shoes to wear and
we should be grateful, etc., to which his son ill-advisedly
replies, "Goody goody gumdrops."

This particular morning I am not up to the spanking,
the tears, or the facial contortions. I am certain that this
child will have hemorrhoids by the time he's ten if he
doesn't quit gritting his teeth and making straining noises
when I make wardrobe suggestions. So we breakfast to
the thundering of sneakers in the dryer, and I hope that
my reputation as a mother is not solely dependent on this
son's costume today.

In the realm of fashion, I thought boys would be easier.
And perhaps they are. The little girl down the street once
wore her bathing suit almost every day for a year—adding
a leotard and long tights underneath when the weather
turned cold. Although I love to finger delicate smocking
on eyelet pinafores and wonder what it would be like to
debate ponytails versus French braids in the morning before school, I suspect that I wasn't cut out to be the
mother of daughters. I don't think I hold up too well
under the scrutiny of the willowy ingenues that pass my
kitchen window en route to junior high school. They
smile indulgently at my permanent-press jeans hemmed
to the ankle as I retrieve a fallen tricycle from their path.
Their skirts are fashionably long (too long for safe bike
riding), their feet are shod in four-inch wedges or
wooden-sole sandals, their makeup, except for occasional
eyebrow experimentation or lime-green eye shadow, is
lovely. What ever happened to acne? Their mothers assure
me that this total look is not easily achieved. It usually involves fifteen minutes of heated hair curlers, three or four
complete costume changes before breakfast, and at least
one good cry because they have nothing to wear. First-

period gym class is to be avoided at all costs. By afternoon, their self-assurance has worn a little thin as they limp and lurch home on voguish shoes never intended for school playgrounds and concrete corridors. Some of them, however, will persevere and become fashionable women.

I have ambivalent feelings about fashionable women. There are days when I look on them with disdain and truly believe that any woman who has the time to paint not only her fingernails but also her toenails fudge brown needs to reassess her priorities. But just occasionally I long to be one of these chic turbaned creatures.

My own forays into the world of chic were stunted early by corrective oxfords and what could be politely described as sturdy legs. I was also hampered somewhat by a mother who never bought name-brand items. If J. C. Penney made a cheaper model, I wore it. But the corrective shoes stand out in my mind as the real stunners. They were heavy-soled red shoes with two straps across the instep. As a mother, I can now see that they were perfectly sensible shoes for my ten-year-old growing flat feet, but at a time when fashion decreed ballerina slippers, they were indescribably painful. My mother did not respond to the tactics my own sons employ on me, so I was forced to hide my Sunday Mary Janes in a paper sack behind a tree halfway to the school to preserve my self-esteem.

The flat feet and sturdy legs remain with me to discourage any false illusions about what the new look will do for me. This season's boots are patently ridiculous for Texas' climate, but that is not the reason I avoid them. It's the look on the shoe clerk's face when he realizes that the leg of the boot won't go over my calf. I also inherited a good bit of puritan conscience about clothes from my frugal mother. If I indulge myself in the second-floor shoe shop at Neiman's, I do it with full knowledge that in the end,

Cotton Mather's God will dangle me over the pits of hell
saying, "Tell us again why you needed Ferragamos?"

This puritan ethic also prevails when it comes to my
annual trek to the beauty shop. This last year's visit was
disastrous. I walked past the Neiman-Marcus Cuttery
four times before I mustered the courage to go in. Warren
Beatty's *Shampoo* was still fresh in my mind, and the
whole scene of hairdressers in blue jeans with hair-drying
blow guns on their hips made me uneasy. No one seemed
to be in charge, so I stood awkwardly in the middle of the
room until someone noticed me. "Just step back there and
put a smock on, honey. Ralph will take you in a minute."
I entered the small room which he had indicated and immediately wished that it had a back door. By "smock" I
presumed he meant these little nightgown things in a basket. Was I to disrobe completely and put this skimpy costume on, or pull it over my clothes? Seeing hangers on a
rack I opted for removing my blouse only, pulling the
smock on over my skirt and returning self-consciously to
Ralph. Already I had become cowardly about the haircut
and heard myself say, "Just trim off the split ends." He
suggested a little styling and I agreed; hairdressers are
even more intimidating than fashionable women. In the
mirror I spotted another awkward kindred spirit timidly
enter the shop. She too was sent to the smock room and to
my horror emerged wearing my blouse. If I thought I
could have made it past the security guards wearing the
smock, I would gladly have abandoned the garment. Instead I quietly humiliated us both by requesting that she
give it back to me. Is it some sort of comment on the
whole world of fashion that she had confused my short-
sleeved French import with a beauty shop smock?

But it is not just the sturdy legs and the sturdy conscience that save me from the pages of *Vogue*. My chil-

dren have had a profound influence on my wardrobe too. My older son made his first comment on the world of fashion when he was scarcely six months old by losing a diaperful in the lap of my new midi skirt as he bounced on my knee in the presence of friends. I am convinced that mothers of sons have to wear blue jeans longer than mothers of daughters. Most daughters, they tell me, do not come home from school and butt their heads into your thighs before they say hello. I know mothers of daughters who spend time mending hurt feelings, while I must thrust myself between two violent forces determined to rip each other's ears off just to decide who gets to brush his teeth first. I also suspect that little girls use tissues to wipe their noses. One of my sons has graduated to using his sleeve or to making horrible snorting noises, but the other still leaves glistening trails across my denim-covered legs. Do little girls project their bubble gum into their mother's hair while learning to blow bubbles or do they just leave it on the kitchen stool where she'll sit in it?

Occasionally when I do dress less casually, my sons know I'm leaving them and respond accordingly. "Hey, where do you think you're going in those panty hose?" When pressed to select my most beautiful dress, they unanimously vote for a voluminous fuchsia-and-green K-Mart muumuu purchased at the height, or perhaps the breadth, of pregnancy.

With some prompting from their father, they occasionally tell me that I am the most beautiful mama in the world. But lest my ego get the best of me, Drew picks up a photograph of me made only last year and says, "Mom, is this a picture of you when you were young?"

With these sons I am thankfully relieved of the burden of being their model in matters of fashion. My taste is really not on the line when they leave the house, as might be the case with daughters. Their clothing, unlike the starched and sashed dresses of my childhood, is practical and effortless to care for, and I'm gradually learning to stop expecting mature adult responses from them when they're rummaging through the dirty clothes before school in the morning. If wearing a faded orange Texas Longhorn sweatshirt every day for a week enables a five-year-old to face his sometimes cruel peers with confidence, who am I to quibble? Perhaps their senses are sharper than mine. How can I argue with a child who says the green stripes on his pajamas smell funny?

I also know that these clothing battles are often mild forerunners of stronger declarations of independence which we will experience when they reach adolescence. What can these boys possibly do to their hair that will sufficiently offend a mom who has known a bald-headed father, bleached butch-waxed flattops, ducktailed pompadours, and now ponytailed postmen? I can only hope that in the long run they will inherit their father's lack of vanity and forever eschew puka shells, white shoes, mustaches, and hair spray.

I'm not overly optimistic, however; Jack just came roaring through the house singing "Rhinestone Cowboy" and demanded to know where he could get a tattoo before tomorrow.

Food for Thought

"Do your children ever join you at the table when you have guests for dinner?" a childless houseguest asked me recently. I suspect she was thinking romantically, as perhaps I once did, of well-mannered, bright children enjoying the company of adults and absorbing witty repartee not unlike that of the celebrated Algonquin Hotel Round Table.

"No," I replied, "they become beasts if they aren't fed before seven o'clock." I regretted that she would miss the shattering reality of lunch with my children the next day. Their behavior is improving, but civilizing forces have not yet conquered the mealtime scene. I sometimes eat lunch before they get home from school—for several reasons. They habitually peer into the leftovers which comprise my noon meal and say, "Oooh, look, Mama's having gross lunch again." In addition to criticizing my meal, they insist on depositing objectionable things from their own plates on mine. Have you ever tried to eat a bowl of chili surrounded by six grape seeds, some partially chewed apple peel, the black spot off the banana, and two complete sets of bread crusts? As for witty conversation, they raise topics like "If your eyeball got poked out with a

pencil, could they put it back in?" Or, "Mom, you know
that gerbil in Mrs. Davenport's class? Well, he died today
. . . but he vomited first. You should have seen it, man."
If the younger son can't think of anything to top the gerbil story, he announces that he needs to go to the bathroom. Once he has completed his visit, he wants to discuss one of his favorite fantasies. "Hey, Jack," he says,
scrambling back into his chair, "if that poo-poo got after
me and locked me in a closet, I would just flush him
down!" This sends them both into paroxysms of laughter
and usually initiates a good five minutes of thinly disguised bathroom talk. Anyone for dinner?

The dinner meal is a little different. I'm not sure when
these little terrorists got the upper hand, but when you
find yourself seriously negotiating with a three-year-old
on Sunday night as to whether three spoonfuls of homemade vegetable soup and two pieces of lettuce entitle
him to watch fifteen minutes of the forbidden "Six Million
Dollar Man" your camp is surrounded.

I suppose I have to bear the burden of guilt since I eat
more meals with those boys than their father does. But
just when and how did the table become the prime place
of parental manipulation and how did I become a short-
order cook? I suspect some of us got caught in that
transition period when baby first joined us at the table,
but really hadn't enough teeth for the entree. We ac-
commodated him with bread and maybe a few carefully
minced pieces of meat. Before we know it, the baby is
five years old, and we are still spooning his portion of spaghetti sauce into an extra skillet before adding the mushrooms in an attempt to keep the peace.

Pediatricians tell me that obesity is the greatest nutritional problem in America today, so I don't try to stuff my
children. I just insist that they taste everything on their

plates. I erred in making dessert the prize. Now my finest meals are viewed as obstacles to be hurdled in order to win a single Oreo cookie.

The original error, of course, was in letting them think what appeared on their plates was any of their business. I'm certain my own mother never allowed us such liberties. Eating at our house was primarily a survival function. Meals were well balanced, but served with no fanfare. All food served was to be eaten. The helpings were never so bountiful that a clean plate would promote obesity, and dessert was unheard of. I remember many times having to sit at the lunch table after everyone had finished, and watch spinach grow stone-cold. Gagging on one's food would have been regarded as theatrical and simply not tolerated, so I usually had to gulp the cold mass quickly or risk missing the afternoon session of school. Occasionally I escaped by furtively feeding a good bit to the dog beside my chair or by leaving the table with food in my hands in order to clean my platter, but I never once thought to say, "How dare you serve me this yucky stuff?"

Times have changed, of course. My parents were never unyielding authority figures; on the other hand, I don't recall that they routinely sought our opinions. My generation, however, is urged by child-rearing experts to involve our children in the decision-making process in order to promote "self-reliance." As one of my friends wryly put it, "The abuse our parents heaped on us, we now receive once again from our own kids." For good or ill, it makes home life more complicated.

For our parents, nutrition, beyond eating your greens and cleaning your plate, was not an overriding concern. They bought us soft drinks without fear of sugar or cyclamates. We snacked on Vienna sausages (sometimes called Vieenas in my small town so as not to confuse them with any European and therefore suspect delicacy) and sardines and crackers with none of the paranoia that now attacks me each time I contemplate the contents of the hog dog on my son's plate. Our parents were also not so beset by a mass culture of jingle-singing children who, thanks to Saturday morning cartoon sponsors, clamor for ersatz food like Twinkies, Breakfast Squares, or Froot Loops.

However, television cannot be held entirely responsible for children's junk food preferences. Peer pressure has a lot to do with it. Even in my own pretelevision childhood, there was much status attached to sneaking off the school ground at lunchtime to have a syrupy cherry Coke and a basket of greasy fries soaked in catsup or, even better, a "Frito pie," a bag of corn chips with extremely questionable chili spooned right into the bag. I am told by an eleven-year-old on my block that a pocketful of Tic-Tac breath mints is currently essential for acceptance in fifth-grade circles.

TV commercials and peer pressure aside, some of the blame is mine. Serving first-rate, nutritional food can be time-consuming and sometimes expensive. One trip to the grocery store a week won't keep the pantry full of fresh fruit, cheese, and vegetables. And peeling carrots, oranges, and hard-boiled eggs for snacks can keep you in the kitchen the better part of the day. For a while I was a zealot and baked whole wheat bread every week, but the futility of my efforts was painfully clear the day my oldest son said, "Mom, this bologna just doesn't look right on this brown bread." Besides the bologna, I also confess to buying chocolate sandwich cookies for my children partly because they much prefer them to anything homemade, and because I do not find them tempting at all. No one

eats wholesome oatmeal raisin or granola peanut butter
cookies except mothers. For sheer convenience when
we're going out for the evening, I have been known to
apologetically slip a frozen TV dinner in the oven for the
kids. To my chagrin, they ecstatically whoop it up all over
the neighborhood, "TV dinners . . . yippeeeee!"

My husband does little to ameliorate my nutritional
faults. More than once a week, he dashes off to work with
only a cup of coffee while the children sing out after him,
"Daddy's gonna run out of gas today." He never returns
from the supermarket without a large bag of potato chips
and a carton of soda pop. He seldom sits down to a meal
without a fruit jar full of jalapeños, and he thinks a house
without a stock of hard candy is not a home. So why is it
that he is lean and tall, has never had a cavity, and, despite a slight propensity for hypochondria, has never been
ill in all our years of marriage? "Genetically speaking, he
picked good parents," a cardiologist neighbor tells me.

Although we are far from pure in our nutritional practices, I do try to buy as much fresh food as possible, still
bake the whole wheat bread about once a month, and
otherwise spend a heck of a lot of money on "no preserv-
ative" whole-grain breads. Along with "We can't afford
it," "No nutrition" is my standard line in refusing to buy
junk food at the supermarket. I may buy the "empty calo-
rie" Oreos, but I parcel them out grudgingly with admonitions about their destructive effect on teeth. Such nutritional sermonizing, however, has a way of backfiring. My
older son, who has recently become a somewhat hypo-
critical prig, remarked to a neighbor child's mother who
had sheltered and fed him for the afternoon, "Did you
know that these Alpha-Bits we're eating will rot our
teeth?" and "Do you always buy this no-nutrition bread?"

After doing some reading in the overladen nutrition

section of my favorite bookstore, I've discovered that due to an overabundance of conflicting authorities, you can find some support for just about any nutritional philosophy.

But we want our table to be more than a place where we ingest the correct balance of carbohydrates, protein, and amino acids, and for that reason the advice on food rites we like best comes from a man who has no credentials in the field of nutrition, Robert Farrar Capon, an Episcopal priest and father of six children. Capon, a witty and articulate lover of food and life in general, is more concerned with the aesthetics of the table. In his book *The Supper of Lamb* (Doubleday Image paperback), Capon suggests that children need to learn "real" from "phony" in life and that the table is a good place to start. To that end we take our boys to the farmers' market in the spring and summer, where they can see carrots with tops intact, unshucked corn, greens with turnips attached, and beets with unwilted beet greens. Once a year they help harvest a real garden in an East Texas farm where they learn that eggs do not grow on eggplants. They still have no great affection for vegetables, but at least they recognize them; in the future when they are finally bored with peanut butter and jelly sandwiches this knowledge should prove helpful. The fish market is one of their favorite haunts now that they've outgrown their lobster tank nightmares, and occasionally they accompany me to ethnic grocery stores and delicatessens, so I can remind them that some men do not live by processed cheese alone. Once the food is purchased, they participate in or, more often, hamper its preparation. I still believe the basketball that landed in the stir-fried squash was deliberately thrown.

Capon agrees that children need their meals balanced, but adds, "My own feeling is that children need to have their tastes *un*balanced: to have them skewed, driven off dead center, and fastened firmly on the astonishing oddness of the world." As a father of six, he has no illusions about children's tastes. "Given a choice between cheeses, for example, they will skirt the Pont-L'Evêque, the Reblochon, the Appenzeller . . . and head with unerring aim for the prepackaged process slices or supermarket Swiss." To turn their tastes to his advantage, he writes, "If they will not taste, so much the better for us. My wife and I spent years trying to urge teenagers to eat mushrooms until it suddenly dawned on us that, far from being defeated, victory had been handed to us on a china platter." He admits that when it looks as if a favorite dish of his will be in short supply, he adds a few mushrooms, and announces solemnly, "You children really must have a good helping of this; the mushrooms are marvelous."

Our efforts at overcoming our own children's philistine tastes are unappreciated. They accuse me of trying to choke them on the pulp in fresh-squeezed orange juice. They eat hot sausage in the Mexican bakery in Austin, but demand Cheerios at my table. Drew refuses crabmeat which he has helped catch in the Gulf, but wants to know if he can dip his toothbrush in the roach poison on the utility porch. I receive compliments only for the hamburger buns (store-bought), not the hamburger, and I know I am tyrannized when I routinely march broccoli "trees" across my three-year-old's plate and cajole him with "Only a giant could eat this forest." Father Capon comforts me, "Their tastes are their own." With him, I have finally decided that the best thing I can do for my children nutritionally is to "keep their minds open and their palates at least willing to try something new every now and then."

You will know my sons at the communion rail, Father Capon. They will be the ones who ask, before accepting the wafer, "Does it have nuts?"

Drive, They Said

AUTOMOBILES HAVE never interested me much. The consummate fraternity man may still be suffering from the time he offered me a ride to campus in his new Ferrari. "Like my new car?" he asked when I did not comment spontaneously. "Oh, yeah," I said. "It's a Studebaker, isn't it?"

It's not at all surprising that I'm still driving my '65 Chevy. Measuring my days in intervals between carpools is unavoidable, and it seems that an inordinate amount of early childhood development is occurring in the car. My sons disdainfully call my maroon-and-black taxi "the purple hog." My husband says if we keep it long enough, it may regain some class. He's wrong. There can be nothing classy about a car that regularly transports children. Although I may not have succumbed to the Country Squire or Estate Wagon, the interior of the Chevy identifies me as suburban car pooler every time. Childless automobiles do not have three Burger King crowns, empty raisin boxes, wrinkled imperatives from the elementary school about snack fees, a pine cone turkey, and sheets of nursery school tempera paintings (Mackintosh *après* Miró and Klee) which never made the refrigerator door gallery.

Twelve Christmas Seals are pasted on the glove compartment. If the backseat has a slightly gamy smell, it is because a bologna sandwich once got pressed for several days in the fold-down armrest which my sons affectionately call "the horse." An assortment of wadded tissues clutters the floorboard. Some were offered, but seldom used, for runny noses. Others were employed for those deplorable spit baths that I swore I'd never inflict on my own children, but that no mother can resist when her offspring is about to dash for the classroom with ear to ear milk-jelly-toast mustaches. I've alerted Jack to watch for the knobs missing from our car window handles at show-and-tell. The insurance company may be suspicious when I report the radio antenna missing for the third time.

How does it happen? Only another suburban mother or a father who has braved long vacations behind the wheel can appreciate the dangers inherent in compressing the energies of small children in the eight-by-five interior of an automobile.

A child's blue windbreaker flies from the backseat and hangs on my rearview mirror just as I'm trying to maneuver into the left lane of the busy expressway. "Who likes deviled crabs?" yells the curly-haired boy who is crouching dangerously near my accelerator. "Yuk!" comes the earsplitting reply from the four passengers in the backseat. "Who likes roasted meat?" asks the shy little Australian girl who shares my son's locker. She and I have special rapport since apropos of nothing she has said, "I like your ponytail." (I thought of it as a sleek chignon when I left home.) "Roasted meat" is ignored because my son has just yelled, "Who likes throw-up?" causing the boy near the accelerator to bump his head on the rearview mirror in sheer delight. The mirror is askew, but at least the windbreaker falls off. We are on a field trip to the Garden

Center and I'm wondering why I didn't tell the room mother who solicited my assistance that we only have a two-seat Porsche instead of this roomy old Chevrolet.

The field trip is of dubious value. The docent patiently explains the process by which seeds are propagated, mentioning at one point that perhaps even their dogs have assisted in spreading a seed caught in their fur. The two little boys in front of me hear only the word "dog" and begin immediately to demonstrate by flapping their left elbows and making appropriate whooshing noises indicating how their respective dogs go to the bathroom. The lights are dimmed for a lovely film of children planting a garden, but the images on the screen are largely obscured by the inevitable waving hand shadows. A shy-looking little boy behind me is besieged by five very aggressive little girls demanding to be kissed. During the actual tour of the garden area, I am depressed to hear one of my son's kindergarten classmates casually reading words like "bromeliad" and "orchid." My son's reading vocabulary is limited to his own name (preferably spelled backward) and the ubiquitous word *Jaws*.

Determined to get the children home safely and swear off field trips forever, I allow only the child who likes my "ponytail" in the front seat. I explain once again that there will be no throwing, punching, or bouncing in the car since I need the rearview mirror to drive safely. My own son puts it more succinctly: "Cool it, you guys, because my mother will get very nervous and crash this car into a barricade." Once the car has pulled away from Fair Park, four children begin to complain bitterly that we didn't get to see any carnivorous plants; the other two are hotly debating whether *Jaws* has an R or a PG rating. I ply them all with sugarless gum and we make it home without incident.

A friend admitted to me the other day that in the "occupation" space on her grocery store identification card she had written "robot who drives the car for the rest of the family." "That's wishful thinking," I told her. "You can't be a robot unless you've dosed yourself with Equanil before you turn on the ignition." For example, the worst drive I ever made was the rainy day Drew (then about two years old) partially severed his finger in a door-slamming incident. Besides his older brother, we had a neighbor child visiting. No neighbors were home to assist in the drive to the hospital, and to call an ambulance for a finger seemed absurd. I piled the two older children, who were totally insensitive to the trauma, in the backseat. The hysterical, shrieking two-year-old with the macabre floppy finger sat with me in the front. I drove in a blinding rain with one hand on the steering wheel and the other restraining the mangled finger which the child was determined to put in his mouth. No robot could be programmed to handle that.

Besides the horror stories of children who open the rear door of station wagons when you're going sixty miles an hour, there are trivial but no less dangerous distractions. My younger son sometimes thrusts his untied sneakers in my face just as I am making a chancy left turn. "Tie them now!" he demands. On occasion he has suddenly swiveled my head 90 degrees to point out a dead squirrel in the street or a cat in a tree. In an impulsive show of affection, he has also tumbled over my shoulder into my lap. I am not a particularly calm driver even when alone, but add the unpredictability of children and my husband's low tolerance for my driving idiosyncrasies and I arrive at our destination with what feels like a totally fused spinal column. My boys are incapable of traveling more than five miles without getting into a rabbit-kicking fight, which sometimes requires me to drive with one hand while flailing wildly with the other in hopes of making contact with one errant bottom. Calm reason is ineffective on long trips. In my experience, any trip that exceeds two hundred miles requires a spanking. I can drive from Dallas to Austin in relative harmony with my children, but if we're going on to San Antonio, I invariably have to pull off just before San Marcos and spank them both. The tears and outrage take the final toll of their energies and they sleep the rest of the way.

I have new admiration for my own parents, who once made a car trip from Texarkana to Washington and New York—without air conditioning—with my brother and me fighting most of the way. Most of the fights were provoked by my brother's affixing the phrase "just for chuckles" to everything I said. My own son now in similar fashion harasses his sibling with the words "Cookie Monster." The younger child will say, "I need a drink of water." His brother will respond, "Drew needs a Cookie Monster drink of water." The backseat, which we have covered with a baby-crib mattress in the naïve hope that both boys will sleep most of the way, now becomes a wild mass of scrambling arms and legs.

My other objection to car trips with the children is that unless I drive, I am forced to straddle a water jug, assorted bags of fruit, crackers and peanut butter, two coloring books and crayons, and anything else the boys think is inhibiting their space in the backseat. Don't tell me that a station wagon would solve all of that. Some of my friends bought a station wagon for a trip to Colorado with their two boys. They looked forward to the peaceful drive with the boys on the foam mattress with their favorite toys in the rear of the automobile. Twenty miles out of town both children were wedged between parents in the front seat, where they remained the rest of the trip.

If the fighting, the food spilled in the car, and the ill-timed bathroom stops don't get you, the "How far is it now?" whining will. My brother devised a plan he says is effective with his daughter. At the beginning of the trip, he gives her twenty nickels. Each time she asks the distance from the destination, she forfeits a nickel. My children would drop all the nickels between the seats.

I am told that the long car trips will improve as the children learn to read or play games without supervision, but that the car pooling gets worse. There will be more of it, the distances from home will be greater, and the boys will be bigger, clumsier, and, after soccer matches, smellier. One mother warns me that at some point her children's friends stopped using the car doors to enter and exit. They use windows, and she has despaired of ever having all the windows up on her car when a rainstorm hits. My children still use the doors, but they usually leave them open. More than once I have had a battery recharged because "the rotten egg" failed to close the door. A friend in San Antonio tells me that his children also fail to close car doors. Once when he came home from work and found the door to the station wagon open, he shut it without bothering to check for occupants. A neighbor's German shepherd had crawled in the car for a nap, and by the time the half-crazed animal was found the next morning, he had shredded every inch of upholstery in the automobile.

In the midst of this peril, I can still think of a redeeming feature to chauffeuring children: the eavesdropping privilege. My older son gives me a pained expression when I casually ask, "School okay today? Do anything special?" But with his friends in the car, I learn all I need to know, not only about school, but also about the social pecking order. I am reassured to hear that children other than my own say, "Stud, man, neato!" and "Aw *right*" (a phrase indicating strong approval, pronounced with what I call athletic inflection). I may hear heated theological debates on "Is God the boss of everything?" or affirmations that George Washington is still alive. They currently have grave doubts about the credibility of Abraham Lincoln, but Santa Claus is still secure. If I listen carefully, I may trace the source of "brung" or "seen him when he dunnit" or perhaps root out the culprit who taught my son the word "nigger." I hear the doggerel of my own childhood mysteriously surfacing in another generation. "Missed me, missed me, now you gotta kiss me," taunts the five-year-old siren who has just deflected a foot intended for her back. Or to a new child in the car pool, "Say dollar." "Dollar," the innocent says. "Pull down your pants and holler," the backseat crowd choruses. And finally those fight-provoking rhymes, "Robin and Peter sitting in a tree/K-I-S-S-I-N-G./First comes love/then comes marriage/then comes Peter in a baby carriage./ Sucking his thumb/wetting his pants/trying to do the hula dance." Comparative anatomy is discussed with nary a blush by this backseat set. "Of course I don't have a penis," a petite four-year-old blonde with go-go boots once informed my son as I double-clutched at the intersection. "Girls have baginas." "Unh-Unh," my son challenged. "My mom is a girl, and she does *not* have any 'bajamas'; she wears a gown."

I might have missed that in a Ferrari.

Tube or Not Tube

WHILE WAITING in a particularly long check-out line at the supermarket the other day, it occurred to me that a discernible pecking order exists among mothers. I was idly sizing up the woman in front of me on the basis of her grocery cart contents. Freakies and Pop Tarts. Hmmmm, probably sleeps late and watches the soaps and sends her son to school with a lunchboxful of Hostess Twinkies, which he trades for my son's fresh banana. But glancing over my shoulder, I couldn't help noticing that my Morton's frozen doughnuts were being smugly regarded by a woman whose cart contained a bag of whole-grain flour, six cartons of yogurt, and four packages of yeast.

The pecking order, of course, is not confined to nutrition. Breast-feeding mothers look askance at those who don't. Pacifist mothers frown on mothers whose children bestow G.I. Joe dolls at birthday parties. Feminist mothers raise their eyebrows at mothers who purchase bosomy Barbie and her beauty shop for their daughters. Early-rising mothers smile self-righteously at nine-thirty Saturday morning when a neighbor's lisping two-year-old, barely heard above the din of the cartoons, answers the phone, "Mama gone night-night."

A mother's approach to television regulation also reflects her position in the pecking order. Somewhere around the bottom of the order is the woman who unashamedly views the tube as her children's nonprescription sedative, a companion to her Valium. The kids have a set in their rooms and have never missed "Gilligan's Island" or "Hong Kong Phooey." At the opposite extreme, of course, is the mother who churns her own butter and claims that her children *never* watch television; they're much too busy reading the *Iliad* or building a Mongolian yurt in the backyard.

Finding my own niche in the pecking order is not easy. I am awed in the presence of mothers whose children snack on dried apricots and soy nuts and who have never heard of "Speed Racer," but I am saved from total ignominy by sugarless gum, hot breakfasts three times a week, "Sesame Street," "Zoom," "Misterogers," and a respectable burden of guilt about "Cartoon Carnival." I do not have to read the Surgeon General's report on the impact of television violence on children's behavior. There are adequate data in my own household to prick my conscience. For example, one afternoon an errand required that we park our car in an underground parking garage (the sort of garage Cannon and Mannix long ago learned to avoid). The headlights of the car parked next to ours had been left on, so, in neighborly fashion, I opened the unlocked car to save the stranger's battery. "Don't, Mom!" Jack shrieked. "Someone will think you're planting a bomb." Does my son have a peculiarly criminal imagination, or do other children routinely build "assassins' cars" and "homing robots" with their Legos building bricks? I made a point to tune in more carefully the next time his friends gathered at our house. Sure enough when a disagreement occurred, I heard one small boy announce, "I'm

going to get the police to put you in jail." "Well," replied
the offender, "police get killed sometimes. If they lock me
up, I'll just make a bomb and set it for ten minutes, then
boom!"

In a *Ladies' Home Journal* article several months ago
(for the pecking-order record, I do not subscribe; I read
it at the library), psychotherapist Victor B. Cline suggested the danger lies not so much in the fact that television may prompt children to emulate violence as in the
emotional blunting that TV violence produces. He indicts
television for the bystander apathy that seems to thwart
urban crime control. Studies for the Surgeon General's
Scientific Advisory Committee on Television and Social
Behavior showed that "the average cartoon hour had
nearly six times the violence rate of the average adult television drama hour."

Television characters figure prominently in children's
fears. Even public television is culpable. "Sesame Street's"
Cookie Monster threatens, but not so much as a sequence
about a seemingly disembodied hand trying to entertain
itself. I have had to exorcise Sam, the Sesame Street
Robot, and Misterogers' People from Planet Purple from
my children's nightmares just as frequently as Felix the
Cat's Master Cylinder.

Television commercials surrounding children's pro-
gramming have probably prompted more organized action from mothers than TV violence. Pitting a two-year-
old child in an intellectual contest against an American
ad agency is reprehensible. I have no defense against allowing a stranger to hard-sell my children on the sugary
cereals or a Snoopy pencil sharpener, but I can retain a
shred of integrity by refusing to buy. And there is one
cynical advantage to be gained by exposing children to
commercials. As an acquaintance remarked, "Probably

one of the most useful lessons an American child can learn early is that people may lie when they're trying to sell you something."

My husband and I are not really of the television generation, but we each recall commercials that trapped us even though we were almost adolescents before our families had TVs. My husband admits to purchasing a Veg-o-matic multipurpose chopper and, with some embarrassment, a Winky Dink kit. Winky Dink, a cartoon character, was always receiving secret messages that the viewer could decode only if he placed the Winky Dink plastic paper over his viewing screen and filled in the necessary lines with a Winky Dink crayon. I succumbed to Revlon, sponsor of "The Sixty-Four Thousand Dollar Question." Remember Snow Peach lipstick and Futurama cases? Slightly bony, but nevertheless glamorous, Barbara Britton lounging in harem costume beside oriental pools with lips and nails painted Persian Melon kept my allowance constantly depleted. Small wonder that my son leans forward on his elbows at the breakfast table before I've had my first cup of coffee and asks somberly, "Mom, do we count on Mutual of Omaha?"

No parent can look at a group of children glaze-eyed in front of the television set ("safely stupefied," as John Updike describes them in *A Month of Sundays*) and doubt that an overdose of the tube is physically and probably mentally debilitating. That television is creating a nation of sluggish spectators scarcely bears repeating. More interesting perhaps is the speculation that television appeals to the right hemisphere of the brain, the portion reputedly least given to logic, while people who depend on the print medium for information use the more methodical left hemisphere. Douglas Cater noted this observation in an article for *Saturday Review* and cited surveys indicating that the more dependent someone becomes on television as a source of information, the more likely he is to feel that he cannot understand or affect the political process. British-American journalist Alistair Cooke underscored that idea in an interview for *U. S. News & World Report,* suggesting that we are overwhelmed with images and unable to make judgments because TV makes us so continuously aware of disruption everywhere. Cooke also bemoans our declining grasp of the English language. He notes that a whole generation, thanks to television commercials, is growing up with pointless "genteelisms" like "moisturize" instead of "moisten" or "dentifrice" instead of "toothpaste."

So why, in the face of these overwhelming indictments, don't we throw the tube out? We tried, but failed. Shortly after the parking lot episode, I announced the cold turkey policy: *no television.* There were withdrawal symptoms, starting with a lot of whining and much talk of "mean old Mother." So Mean Old Mother made feeble attempts at becoming Supermom. We went to the library twice a week and boned up on dozens of books about rainy-day entertainment of children. These suggestions always seemed to call for "simple common household items" that are simply not common in my house. I don't buy margarine in tubs or eggs in Styrofoam cartons, and the wood scraps left from our house expansion were burned in the fireplace last winter. So we spent at least five dollars (the cost of a Batmobile, my son reminded me) purchasing "common household items" like string, nails, and butcher paper, and drove halfway across town for lumberyard scraps. But all the projects were doomed to failure, primarily because they were instigated by Mom. My children's creativity instead was directed toward getting invited to neighbors' houses at preschoolers' prime time in order to see "Speed Racer," a cartoon described by the *Guide to Children's Television* as "virulently violent." The hour before dinner became a nightmare of siblings bickering and begging for bread and circuses. "You got chicken blood on the cards," Jack wailed as I tried to prepare dinner and play Go Fish at the same time.

By the end of the week, I had resorted to bribery: Legos. This toy, created in Denmark, is a set of small plastic bricks that may be assembled in ingenious ways that the makers of Tinker Toys never imagined. Perhaps because my older son has always been a builder and has never allowed his brother to be anything else, Legos are extremely absorbing toys at our house. Unfortunately, they are also ridiculously expensive and are sold only in boxed sets. After a week of building, my son determined that he had to have some "slopy pieces," which are contained only in the set that retails for $25.95. When I explained that we couldn't afford the desired pieces, he responded thoughtfully, "Mom, I guess we just don't have enough money to do without TV."

Before the second week of our experiment was over, we had returned to modified television viewing of PBS programs and occasionally "Captain Kangaroo." After one week of abstention, my husband and I could no longer tolerate our growing self-righteousness, particularly in view of our apparent hypocrisy. Though we read, work, or talk many more evenings than we watch television, alert youngsters out of their beds for another drink of water once caught their work-dazed father watching "Hawaii Five-O." "Stuffing your head with candy, Dad?" Jack taunted.

After our brief experiment, we confess that we have ambivalent feelings about television for children. Aside from air conditioning, it is the most inescapable difference in our own childhood and that of our children. We have no inherited patterns from our own parents to prescribe its use. We cannot deny that television has broadened our children's horizons and vocabularies. From time to time we regret that we can take so little credit for their apparent precocity. Overhearing my conversation about a friend's ill mother who could no longer eat, Jack piped up authoritatively, "Couldn't the doctor just feed her intravenously?" His talk of oxygen, anesthetics, and surgical technique comes from regular ambulance chasing on NBC's "Emergency," not from his parents. When I chaperone their kindergarten class to the zoo, he and his classmates point out iguanas, coatimundis, toucans, and tapirs—their friends from "Captain Kangaroo"—while I insult the chimpanzee by ignorantly calling him a monkey.

Public service messages on television often lend credence to our parental admonitions, although I suspect our friends who smoke wish my son would ease up on the talk of emphysema and wheelchairs. He has perhaps also gone overboard on the protection of the environment. "You know, Mom," he announced one morning, "I think we're going to have to stop using the toilet." "Why?" I asked, fearing another pair of training pants down the pipes. "Well, that stuff has to go somewhere, and I think it's polluting our rivers and streams."

So much for my rationalizing. The truth is that Mother needs a breather, too, and my son pegged it correctly when he said during one particularly rocky afternoon, "Mom, don't you know, watching TV makes me have patience." Although I try not to abuse its sedative effects, television has permitted me some important and pleasant uninterrupted adult conversations. The day both boys awoke at seven, screaming with ear infections and we could not see a doctor until nine-thirty, the Saturday-

morning cartoons tranquilized them as no amount of
rocking by Mom could have done. Thirty minutes of pas-
sive "Sesame Street" watching in the afternoon can head
off vivid displays of violence between brothers, or perhaps between mother and son.

So I'm pursuing a moderate course, occasionally feeling
guilty about being a mother of flimsy—more comfortably
known as flexible—conviction. My sons were never total
TV addicts until I made it forbidden fruit, anyway. Our
modified plan leans heavily toward Public Television, although I realize, of course, that there is an element of
truth in Colman McCarthy's *Newsweek* essay "Ousting
the Stranger from the House." McCarthy sees these "quality" shows as a "moral hustle, conning parents into thinking it's high educational experience to dump the kids before the tube."

We concede there is little advantage in a child's being
able to parrot numbers and letters when he still can't tie
his own shoes. On the other hand, we have watched
enough "Sesame Street" and the like to know that these
shows often prompt creative activity and introduce our
children to people of varied backgrounds whom they
would certainly never meet growing up in our Waspy
neighborhood.

We are even permitting occasional cartoons. I'm convinced that Bugs Bunny is not inflicting serious harm
when I hear my children laughing out loud. My husband,
against my better judgment, is relieved to have "The
Three Stooges" back again from time to time. I am ada-
mant, however, that our television set will not become
"audible wallpaper" as Alistair Cooke describes it, and I
insist that the set be turned off when no one is watching.

Now that my miniwar with the one-eyed monster is
over, we're quietly reading J. M. Barrie's *Peter Pan* aloud

to Jack. The look of wonder in his eyes as we read about fairies being born out of baby laughter reassures me that television even at its very best has a long way to go before it seriously threatens the written word.

Part Two

Something Happened

I WAS GLAD I had brought my sunglasses. First-graders don't cry anymore on that first day of school, but mothers do. Most of the children I know have been in some sort of school since they were three years old, so being away from their mothers is nothing new. However, perhaps because the first grade with its required smallpox scabs, book satchels, and new crayons was more momentous in our own lives, we tend to insist that it be some sort of milestone for our offspring. My boys' growing independence does not threaten me particularly. We've long had a self-congratulatory game around here called "I don't need a mother to open the car door, buckle my belt, pour my milk, etc. . . ." The longer the list, the prouder the boy, and the more time Mom has to read *Shōgun*. I did not weep over my worthlessness the day "tie my shoes" and "wipe my bottom" were added to their respective lists.

So why did I need the sunglasses today? Walking home, I tried to account for my tears. I certainly didn't want him to come home with me, and I'm sure I would have wept longer if he had clung to my skirt at the door. Indeed, during the dog days of August, I would have gladly handed both boys off to the first unsuspecting grandmotherly sort in the grocery store who foolishly admired them and said, "Why don't you boys just come home with me?" In August their bickering reached such a pitch that no one even offered. Twice that month I stopped the car and ordered them to the backseat, once instructing them to go ahead and fight until someone bled (they chickened out), and another time making them walk barefoot on the hot sidewalk for a block on the way to the swimming pool until they agreed to cut out the squabbling. No, I don't really want him to come home with me.

Maybe the tears fell, not because I feared the letting go, but because this child has never really been mine. He has my physical features—large eyes, stocky legs, and flat feet—but lacks my pacifist nature. He has never forgiven me for selling his bayonet-bearing soldiers in the garage sale. And he consistently resists any impositions of my taste on his. For his birthdays and Christmas, I have purchased beautiful books like *The Red Balloon* by A. Lamorisse, Marguerite Henry's *Birds at Home,* or Robert McCloskey's *Time of Wonder.* They collect dust. Or even worse, he hauls them out to the garage sale to make money to purchase a missile-firing army tank. The cabinet is filled with records like "Peter and the Wolf," "Carnival of the Animals," Benjamin Britten's "Young Person's Guide to the Orchestra," and even gentle Mister Rogers' "You Are Special." I listen to them, but he prefers "La Bamba." I bought neat striped rugby shirts for school this year, but allowed him to select one shirt on his own. His choice has cartoon characters with their tongues hanging out, who stomp on each other or sit astride motorcycles. He's wearing it today, and I'm sure his first-grade teacher has duly noted it and arbitrarily assigned him to the slow reading group. He is attracted to kids named Bubba or Butch who talk about "rippin' off Cokes." And when he goes for a visit with a child whose influence is more to my liking—you know, the bilingual kid who collects stamps and watches birds—he returns with this report: "Yeah, I had a tons good time. He has the neatest stuff in his room —a calculator and a tape recorder. You know what I recorded on the tape?" "No, what?" I asked, hoping for "Row, Row, Row Your Boat." "I said, 'ladies' boobs, ladies' boobs, ladies' boobs' until we fell down laughing." "What is so funny about ladies' boots?" I asked, certain that he had developed a speech impediment. "No, Mom, boobies, and Kev said that he was going to play it for his daddy tonight."

I try hard to share some of his interests, but I can only say so much about CB radios, Corvette Stringrays, and Donny and Marie. If he really does become a race car driver or a "star" like KC of KC and the Sunshine Band of disco fame as he often tells me he will, I wonder if we'll even want to know each other when he's grown.

His slangy conversation reveals that he is now more the product of his peers than that of his parents. He's always been a gregarious child, but the first real signs of his new allegiances appeared last spring. The vacant lot across the street lured every male child in the neighborhood. Clubs with names like the Dallas Rednecks or Motocross Madmen were formed with secret initiation rites. "Don't worry, Mom," Jack assured me. "Our club is mainly a spears-and-knives club." He later told me that to gain acceptance in the best club, the older boys' pack, it had been necessary for him to learn the Cub Scout pledge, sing in its entirety "99 Bottles of Beer on the Wall," climb on a thin limb of a pecan tree, belch loud enough to be heard in the alley, and show his underwear. Because he was the youngest member and undoubtedly the least welcome, I suspected that his elders would find a way to eliminate him before the week was out. Sure enough, one afternoon he came crying and hiccuping back into our yard and insisted that I talk with him in private. Between the tearful gulps, he blurted out, "Gary and Wayne [the big boys] are saying 'Sick, sick, sick, Jack eats do-do.' Make 'em stop, Mama, make 'em stop!" Seasoned by six years with little boys and recalling the torments of my older brother, I envisioned a new devilish initiation rite. "Well, did you?" I asked. "Yes," he answered with another gush of tears, "but I didn't know what it was. See, we were building a new fort, and I picked up this board that had something on it, and I didn't know what it was, and I wiped it on my jeans, but it wouldn't come off, so I stuck my finger in my mouth, and that's when they said I ate do-do, and they're gonna tell everybody in the world, and everybody will say 'Sick, sick, sick' when they see me." I remembered the pain of these childhood humiliations and knew that his tears were probably justified. I can still recall the name of the girl in my second-grade class who wet her pants on the monkey bars during recess. She does not attend our high school class reunions.

Fortunately the big boys, whom he still idolizes, did not tell the whole world. In fact, their family moved to Albuquerque three weeks later, so I think his reputation is safe. However, he's on his own with the neighborhood bullies from here on out. He still comes running when the bigger boys on dirt bikes destroy his carefully laid highways in the dirt pile on the vacant lot. I give sympathy, but no assistance. And he makes what I know to be empty resolutions like, "When I get to be big, I'll never treat little boys like that."

But today, we set the summer aside. The preparation for this first day of school has been going on for some time. Once during the summer he announced, "Don't buy me any more books with dogs and cats that talk; I just want real books." He ruthlessly proceeded to clear his bookshelves of every fantasy. It occurred to me as I watched the stack of discarded books grow that some of the books I had intended to read to him might never be read now. Had we read enough Mother Goose? Would he never sit still again for the Brothers Grimm tales of trolls, witches, and wishes? Would his imagination from here on out be fueled only by Kojak and Batman? Once the bookcase was arranged, he turned his attention to the pictures that have decorated his wall for six years. "What are we going to do about all this baby stuff?" he asked, taking down Raggedy Andy, a lovingly cross-stitched Hickory Dickory Dock picture, and a poster from the Eeyore's Birthday Party staged in New York's Central Park the year he was born. Later the same day, he dragged a long piece of scrap lumber from the lot across the street and announced, "If you're not going to get my brother out of my room, I'll just have to do this." The plank now divides the room in half. That evening when I suggested that both boys take baths before dinner, he was outraged. "Don't you know that only babies eat dinner in their pajamas?" He is full of slightly sarcastic phrases like "For your information" and "Have you ever heard of. . . ."

Because he attended public kindergarten last year, I suppose he is more or less prepared for the first grade. He can tie his shoes, cross streets, recite his address and telephone number, although he still formally addresses me as "Mrs. Mackintosh" when he calls on the phone. He knows where the school cafeteria and bathrooms are. He's glad that he learned last year that nobody drops his pants at the urinal in the boys' restroom. There are some things a mother forgets to tell you.

The kindergarten year was good preparation for me, too. Public school brings the scrutiny of another adult who sees your child as one among twenty-two. Where you have seen him as remarkably wise, she notes that he is often distracted during "circle time." Where you have sensed unique perception, she observes that he has a right-to-left orientation. And where you think you have been exceptionally tolerant and not at all pushy, she suggests that perhaps he is under pressure at home. For the first time your quality as a parent is formally called into question, and, although you know better, the guilt floods in.

School is also where girls become unavoidable. Although he does not include them in his birthday parties and generally views them with contempt, he is a little puzzled by their amazing manipulative power. I have seen little girls in our backyard transform a simple game of tag by issuing new commands like, "Okay, girls chase boys!" "Now it's boys kiss girls!" The little boys seem to hate the kissing part, but comply because the girls demand it. Even in kindergarten, my son was well aware of "Dawn, the most beautiful girl in our class, who doesn't love me." Dawn's mother informs me that her daughter had my son pegged as "gross" early in the year, but has lately referred to him as a gentleman. Jack is also a little awed by girls' superior physical coordination at this age. Returning from a birthday party, he asked, "Mom, why is it that girls can just put on skates and skate without falling down? They just jump in the water and start swimming, too." About that time three seven-year-old girls came breezing down the street on their bikes with "no hands." They deliberately ignored him. "How'd they grow up before me?" he wonders out loud. "They used to be little bitty old girls."

Although he and his brother try the limits of our endurance from time to time, I'm glad that their letting go is such a gradual process. In the meantime, they continue to force a certain amount of maturity, unselfishness, and courage on us. Nothing frightens them so much as my vulnerability; nothing annoys them more than my shortcomings. Jack is the keeper of my humility. My housekeeping abilities fall far below his standards. "Oh, we have tons of bugs in this house," I overhear him telling friends who are delighted by a noisy cricket in his closet. When his brother spies a favorite, but hopelessly ripped, shirt now consigned to the rag bag and sets up a howl, it is Jack who rebukes me: "Haven't you ever heard of sewing?" But best of all, he keeps us laughing. Recently his attorney father was so involved in a lengthy trial that he felt compelled to explain to the boys the intricate details of the lawsuit in hopes that they would understand why he was spending so little time with them. He emerged from the courthouse victorious at the end of the week and reported, "I won my lawsuit!" Jack responded, "Does it fit you?"

When Jack comes home this afternoon, I know better than to quiz him about his day. As a final declaration of maturity, he insisted that we also move the much-used rocking chair out of his bedroom and into what will be the new baby's room. In its place is a school desk. We may not ever move the rocking chair back, but I suspect we'll sit there together again. It was a good place to discuss preschool anxieties like "What if everybody else has lost their teeth over the summer and I'm the only one with mine still tight?" or "Do you really think the coach makes first-graders run for an hour till their stomachs hurt?" And there are still fears to be worked out about skeletons and robots and why he doesn't want to go on the Mini Mine Train at Six Flags Amusement Park again or see Walt Disney's *Treasure of Matecumbe*. The child-rearing experts tell me that the first six years are the crucial ones, but I don't think we're out of business yet.

It's Better to Receive

I KNOW THAT my Christmas expectations are unrealistic. I want traditions, candles, snow, fresh green trees, Advent wreaths, music, pageants, stories, blazing puddings, clan gatherings, and selfless giving.

My sons want an Evel Knievel Stunt Cycle.

"They're boys, Prudence," my husband reminds me and admits that his own most vivid Christmas memories revolve not so much around the smell of fruitcakes or sounds of "Silent Night" as around the counting up of loot on Christmas morning. Why do I expect some sort of heightened sensitivity from my children in December when only two months earlier on hearing a Raggedy Ann story on the radio, they had asked, "Mom, if that doll really has a candy heart, why doesn't somebody just rip it out and eat it?"

And how could I forget last Christmas? Several weeks before the holiday, I came across *Take Joy*, a lovely Christmas anthology by Tasha Tudor. Certain that my boys (then ages five and three) were old enough to be immersed in Christmas stories, legends, and poems that could become part of our family's holiday tradition, I bought the book and rushed home to make it the first gift

of the season. Their dawdling in the bathtub that evening
was cut short when I announced that they could open a
very special present as soon as they had their pajamas on.
"This is a present for the whole family," I hinted. "Oh, I
know what it is! I know! I know!" the five-year-old, who
has total recall of every Channel 11 television commercial, squealed. "It must be a Ronco Rhinestone Stud Set-
ter, you know, 'Fun for the whole family.'" My heart
began to sink. Sure enough, when the wrappings were
shredded in front of the fireplace, both children responded, "Oooh, gross, it's a book. I thought you said it
was gonna be something neat." "But we can read some of
it every night until Christmas, and we can make the
cookies and sing the songs and be Kris Kringles," I
protested. "Forget it, Mom, give it to those people who
don't get anything for Christmas. What made you think
me and Drew would like a crummy old book?" Jack said,
dropping my Yuletide aspirations with the wadded paper
and ribbon on the floor. They were off to bed, no doubt to
say prayers that Santa would not consult their mother before dropping the Evel Knievel Stunt Cycle down our
chimney.

But what would my sons have to remember about their
childhood Christmases beside resolute greed? Would they
remember the food? Not these philistines, who refrigerate
their hot chocolate and eat the marshmallows separately
and who prefer Oreos to homemade gingerbread men.
But then, what memories do I have of Christmas goodies?
Selfless giving was, and is still, my mother's strong point,
and she never felt that that had anything to do with
stuffing her own family with Christmas baking. Besides,
how many children really like fruitcake and rum balls?
Had the Christmas feast been prepared at our house,

Colonel Sanders would have had to cater. We gathered instead at a cousin's house, and I'm fairly certain that I picked the onions out of the corn-bread dressing on my plate, complained about dark meat, shuddered over giblet gravy, and tried to fill up on bakery rolls. I'm sure I asked to be excused before the mincemeat or pumpkin pies were served. A taste for such delicacies is rarely acquired by age six.

Perhaps my sons would remember the Christmas music. Public school, for good or ill, will probably see to it that Jack memorizes the standard carols this year, but Drew consistently replaces my Handel recordings and even my "lords a-leaping" with Janis Joplin. My own strong associations of Christmas with music probably have more to do with participation in choirs and little-girl longings to be a blond soprano Christmas angel in a flowing white gown than with musical experiences my parents foisted on me at home. My father, however, has been known to do a fair Yuletide medley while shaving in December.

The Christmas tree is pretty important to the boys, despite the fact that the annual pilgrimage to the Christmas tree lots with their father, who is determined to get the best deal, usually ends in tears of exhaustion. I've given them special ornaments each year and allowed all the nursery-school decorations to be prominently displayed, but what they seem to remember best are the words their daddy uses to get the tree jammed into the tree stand. But then, there were no particularly memorable trees in my childhood. I'm quite sure, had they been available, my very practical mother would have been the first on our block to purchase an artificial tree. Our decorations were always dime-store bought with little sentiment attached. Funny that I should become the sort of mother who packs each little handmade ornament away in tissue paper and expects her children to be overwhelmed with nostalgia when they are unwrapped the following year.

As for clan gatherings, our immediate family is rather small—two grandmothers, a grandfather, sometimes a great-aunt, and, until this year, a great-grandfather. The gatherings are probably the most romanticized part of my childhood Christmas memories. Looking back over the Christmases I can remember, I see them as a blur of Uncle Burton telling stories about dogs who ate okra, red-vested Cousin Charlie serving old-fashioneds to the grown-ups with a "ho-ho-ho," Aunt Lois cackling appreciatively at my brother's impersonations, and, best of all, visits with our Clarksville cousins, the Marables. The Marable family, headed then by my great-aunt Mattie, a matriarch with a palsied voice, were the loudest, grandest grown-up people I had ever seen. All seven brothers and sisters played musical instruments and sang in four-part harmony. Stories about their childhood improved with each year's raucous and frequently interrupted telling. My young Clarksville cousins were expected to put on a pageant for the adults each year, and I vividly remember a small bathrobed shepherd consulting his new Christmas watch before making much of his line, "Lo, we must go *with haste* to Bethlehem to see this thing which has come to pass." It's impossible to know if I really enjoyed these holiday gatherings as a child as much as I like to think I did. As an eight-year-old did I perhaps whine, "When are we going home?" Or as an adolescent was I embarrassed by everyone's uninhibited outpouring of affection?

Will my sons have any memories of our small gatherings? Their experiences are not at all like mine, but certainly they won't forget the Christmases spent with their great-grandfather, Fred Porter, whom they called "Papa."

His holiday visits to our house received much advance billing by my sons. By the time he arrived, a dozen or so little boys from the neighborhood were on hand to see "the oldest man in the world." He was eighty-six when my older son was born. Not many boys born in 1970 will be able to say that they knew someone who played the cornet in the U. S. Army Band stationed in the Philippines just after the Spanish-American War. But history is not impressive to these little boys. They were far more interested in the eccentricities of this grand old personality. They eagerly carried his suitcase to our guest room and would later ask me why he called it a "grip." His false teeth were a never-ending source of fascination for the boys. I don't know if he ever permitted them to try his dentures on, but I do know that the teeth spent a good part of the visit out of his mouth. Jack and Drew also experimented with wearing several pairs of socks and two shirts because "Papa does." In good weather they took walks with him along Turtle Creek and loved his "jogging," which mainly involved lifting his feet a little higher—no faster—and swinging his arms as if he were sprinting. Even a three-year-old could keep up with him. In fact he often said he had great rapport with Drew, because "we both sometimes have bathroom accidents, and we have to take naps."

He ordered these sons of mine around like a drill sergeant. They were dispatched to fetch pipes, matches, tobacco, newspapers, and they were his most obedient servants. They somehow knew instinctively that he was a father from an age when children did as they were told. They also learned quickly that Papa did not think much of little boys who cried. After five years of being an enlightened mother who teaches males that it is perfectly all right to cry, I was secretly relieved to hear Papa occasionally growl "Crybaby" at them. A skinned knee or a splinter seldom merits the tearful performance we routinely get around here.

His Christmas visits were enhanced by Papa's constant companion, Siggi, a black mongrel also known as the Senator when he performed on his hind legs and ate like a gentleman at the table. Siggi, much to the boys' delight, had slept with Papa for nearly fifteen years and thrived on a diet supplemented by malted milk balls (part of his act required his catching them in midair) and remnants of Morton's macaroni and cheese dinners served in the aluminum pie tin so lightweight that the poor dog frequently had to pursue it all over the kitchen floor while the boys shrieked, "Get it, Sig!"

My boys also instinctively knew that Papa was a man's man. He might play the piano with his stiff old fingers and harmonize on "Silent Night" with their mom occasionally, but it was his bedside table that really defined him for them. He always had within easy reach small pliers, screwdrivers, a flashlight, nail clippers, pocket knives, rubber bands, homemade tobacco pouches that he had stitched up himself on an ancient treadle sewing machine, cigar boxes of old pictures and postcards, assorted sizes of fishhooks, leader, and lead weights, .22 cartridges, Anacin, Alka-Seltzer, and Campho-Phenique, which he regarded as panaceas for all ailments, scentless Vicks inhalers, a couple of cigarette lighters, pipe cleaners, screws, small tacks, and a myriad of other sundries. He growled at the kids if they fingered anything on his table, but was delighted that they had some interest in manual skills.

Even his death at age ninety-two this past winter did little to diminish my boys' curiosity about Papa. The pleasure of his presence in their brief memories causes

Drew to ask, "Can Papa still do his knuckles like this?" or "Is Siggi still jealous because Papa loves me the best?" Jack wanted to know in October what I planned to do about Papa's Christmas stocking. Because the birth of a third baby in November will seriously undermine any elaborate plans for Christmas this year, I didn't postpone this discussion until December. Instead we got out the stockings. The one with the little black felt dog and the dime-store pipe sewn on it made me blink hard. "I know, Mom," Jack says, "we can just take the Siggi and stuff off Papa's stocking and put something for the new baby on it." He still knows his great-grandfather well: Fred Porter certainly wouldn't countenance our throwing anything out.

Their conversation about Papa and stockings leads quickly to Christmas wish lists and overconfident remarks about a Santa who will leave Swiss Army knives in Christmas stockings. My husband is right. They aren't girls, and they are very young. Evel Knievel has a lot more appeal than a Christmas crèche at this point in their lives. And their Christmases are not entirely mine to create. The characters and experiences they bring to the holiday are very different from the ones I knew as a child. It will be just my luck if after twenty years of my Christmas baking, decorating, and singing, their fondest memory is of Christmas 1976, the year the new baby had colic, and we ordered Christmas dinner from the Highland Park Cafeteria.

Birth of a Notion

A LOT OF things had changed in the four years since I had made a serious visit to the obstetrician. Though certain aspects of having babies seem immutable, I got clues from my doctors, the media, and the attitudes of my friends and family that these nine months would not be a rerun of previous pregnancies. For one thing, in the interim since my last childbirth my first obstetrician had gone into gynecology exclusively. "I just got tired of women telling me how to deliver their babies," he confessed. The last straw, he said, was a woman who wanted him to squat beneath her in a foxhole so she could deliver *au naturel.*

I liked his candor, and I had grown accustomed to his phony French Provincial reception room. The inner sanctum, except for a powder room with a gold-leaf mirror and a lavatory with dolphin fixtures, was pleasantly functional. He had a nurse who "honeyed" or "sweetied" everyone right through menopause. I always figured that she had begun her career in pediatrics, since she always said, "Just take your little panties off and the doctor will see you in a minute." His receptionist, who frequently diagnosed over the phone, adored gynecological gossip.

("Just a minute, hon, Mrs. Peters is on the other line—thinks her IUD has slipped.")

My new obstetricians' office would take some getting used to. These fellows—hardly anyone ever tackles obstetrics alone these days—were a little younger, and their decorator's taste ran to twin porcelain leopards, thick shag carpeting, and low-slung velour couches that no one could use beyond the sixth month. My previous obstetrician's office always had a few "Seven Warning Signals" tracts lying around, but this new place was multimedia. On my first visit, in addition to Mancini's "Moon River" piped over the Muzak, a sound-and-light show was being projected on one wall by an automatic projector. The woman sitting beside me kept shielding her preschooler's eyes and reading *The Cat in the Hat* with increasing volume while the projector assaulted us with close-ups of a woman giving herself a monthly breast check. Whatever happened to the good old days when you could just sit and read "Can This Marriage Be Saved?" in *Ladies' Home Journal?*

The decorator had even invaded the examination rooms. I had an overwhelming sense of déjà vu when I was ushered into the lime-green-and-apricot cubicle on this first visit. Small saloon-type swinging doors designated a tiny dressing room in the corner. When I saw the baby-doll pajama tops with small pink rosebuds, I knew where I'd seen it all before—the swanky beauty shop at Neiman-Marcus. Even the disposable paper on the examination table was flowered. The stirrups wore lavender crocheted booties. The powder room had the same old hot and cold bronze dolphins, but something new had been added. When asked for a urine specimen, I embarrassed everyone by reappearing at the nurses' station with my small jar in hand. "Oh, no," one of them said, taking me back to the powder room. Just above the toilet paper dispenser was a small door. She opened it and instructed me to place the specimen there. A door opened on the other side and an anonymous hand retrieved the jar.

The doctors themselves were different. My attorney husband (who does a good bit of medical malpractice defense work) was satisfied that I had found doctors who were board-certified. However, regardless of credentials, doctors who wear neck jewelry and conceal their receding hairlines by combing their hair forward from the neckline do not inspire confidence in me on the first visit. These new obstetricians, nevertheless, were extremely thorough. Their offices were equipped with every possible modern gynecological doodad. When I told my boys about hearing the fetal heartbeat with the sonic detector, they were not particularly impressed. "We could probably pick up that baby on a CB if you'd get us one," they said. I thought perhaps my doctors' attention to every possible complication might be because I was over thirty this time around. My husband reassured me that it was just what they call "defensive medicine." Frankly, I would rather detect a backache myself than be told at two months that my spinal misalignment would probably make me extremely uncomfortable from the sixth month on. That gave me four months to wait for it to hurt.

There were other factors that made this pregnancy different. None of my close friends were having any more babies. They had taken zero population growth seriously. Some had gone in for tubal ligations and sold their baby cribs at garage sales. They enrolled in exercise classes to banish their cellulite and midriff spare tires. Some had divorced, gone to law school, resumed work on their dissertations; the remainder were now to be seen ignoring their children in the park while they read Gail Sheehy's

Passages trying to decide if they were perpetual "care-givers" or just "nurturers who had deferred achievement." They responded to my news with incredulity and generous offers of maternity clothes. With fashion finally paying some attention to the needs of expectant mothers, I had intended to go this third pregnancy in style—chic caftans, Mexican wedding skirts, and Lady Madonna cool crinkle cottons. However, my puritan frugality won out, and by the eighth month a sudden cold snap reduced me to a couple of borrowed puffed-sleeve polyester pantsuits.

My other children made this experience a little different, too. With the baby due in November, I waited as long as possible to tell my two sons. I made it to the middle of June before my "weird" bathing suit gave me away. Jack, the six-year-old, said, "Are you sure you didn't just eat too much?" And Drew, the four-year-old, queried, "Well, who is it going to be?" With my second pregnancy, I had had to deal only with a lisping two-year-old who occasionally patted my stomach and said, "Baby?" and with my own anxieties about sibling rivalry. This time my boys were old enough to verbalize anxieties of their own. They invited all their friends in to look at my stomach and advanced their sex education by quizzing me at the dinner table. "Does that spaghetti you're eating just fall splat on the baby's head?" "How does the baby's poo-poo get out?" When punished, Jack frequently riposted, "You are not having a baby—you *did* just eat too much and you are fat, fat, fat. And if you do get a baby, you won't love us anymore because you always love new things better." Drew was determined to have a smart baby and was constantly holding up his "Sesame Street" books and whispering to my abdomen, "Hello, Mr. Nobody, are you listening? This is a square. Got it? A square." At night when I tucked them in, the fears sometimes surfaced. "Mama," Jack would say, "did you know that that baby is going to hurt you? I've seen it on *Emergency*. They took this woman to the hospital in the ambulance, and she screamed and screamed." And Drew wanted to know, "Mama, if you die, will this baby be old enough to be our mama?"

One thing that remained unchanged with this pregnancy was the neighborhood swimming pool. Spending several hours a day there is our summer ritual, and nowhere else do I feel more like a character in a John Updike suburban short story. Mothers in overbloused swimsuits slather themselves with Coppertone, spread their beach towels, and establish their territory for the long hot summer. Someone is always pregnant at the wading pool, and though we may not know each other's last names, by August we know each other's complete gynecological histories. Having spent two summers pregnant at the pool, I have observed that we all participate to some extent in what a male friend of mine calls "competitive childbirth." He coined the expression after enduring Lamaze natural childbirth classes with his wife. The competition begins at conception. We compare notes on morning sickness. There is virtue at either end of the spectrum: e.g., "I never felt better in my life," or, "I always puke my guts out for the first three months." After the first trimester we enter the ridiculous phase of "Can you believe she's nearly four months and still getting into her tank suit?" To postpone telling my boys the news, I *did* wear my regular bathing suit to the pool for two weeks in June, but nearly passed out holding my stomach in.

Women never seem to forget how much weight they gained with each pregnancy. Some women have been known to lie about their due dates to avoid those humiliating questions about twins in their family when their stomachs give way in the third month. "Showing" too early can be redeemed, however, by staying on the tennis court or jogging into your ninth month. Once last summer we were invited to a cleverly conceived Olympics party in a nearby park. Being the sedentary sort anyway, I was relieved to have my pregnancy as an obvious excuse to stir the chili and nibble brownies while everyone else did the wheelbarrow relay. On arriving at the party, I was confronted by a woman more pregnant than I who said, "They're trying to make us fix the dinner while they're having all the fun and I won't stand for it. We'll show 'em, won't we, Prudence?" The gauntlet was tossed. I showed them all right, and I still shudder to recall that somewhere there is a home movie of me grass-stained and sweaty doing the duck walk in my sixth month.

At the neighborhood pool, the very presence of a woman in her sixth month elicits obstetrical horror stories or embarrassing intimacies from complete strangers. The conversations may go something like this: "When's your baby due?" "Is this your first?" (That's courtly, or perhaps her sunglassses aren't prescription.) "Two boys, hmmm . . . Trying for your girl? Now, Arnold and I did it by the book, you know, the temperatures and douches and all and we swear by it. I'm sure we would have just kept having girls forever." Another mother may chime in, "Girls? You can have 'em. I thought I wanted one, and now that I've got her, she turns out to be a whiny little snot. I'll take my boys any day, but, as Ronnie says, she'll probably take care of us when we get old."

The mothers of many children will invariably confide, "You know, it's the third one that finally wrecks your body. See these veins? I never had any of that with the first two, but with Alice I gained fifty pounds. Never have been able to get rid of that last twenty. You know, the

older you get, the harder it is." And another: "Don't count
on your labor being shorter with this third one. I had Lisa
and Erik so fast we hardly got to the hospital, but with
Jennifer I just stayed at five centimeters for eight hours."
With all of this gruesome talk, you'd expect our eavesdropping progeny to be unduly sophisticated. I found it
refreshing one afternoon when a five-year-old girl demanded that I give her the beach ball I was hiding under
my suit.

The height of the childbirth competition is, of course,
the delivery. No one ever confesses to being totally
knocked out anymore. Even Cesarean candidates have to
watch. Back in 1970 I was terribly avant-garde with
Lamaze breathing and panting and my husband's presence in the delivery room. I know that's all very standard
now when I overhear people discuss things like Kegel ex-
ercises, cervix, and episiotomy in mixed company who
five years ago wouldn't have said Midol without blushing.
Even the most reluctant husbands are routinely dragged
into the delivery room these days. No, to be out front this
year, you have to deliver nonviolently in the dark to soft
music *à la* Leboyer or at least consider "home delivery"
with a midwife and hordes of supportive female friends
and relatives. Men, I think, are no longer welcome, since
this is supposed to be a female bonding experience.

Actually, I find the common experiences and shared in-
dignities at the hospital—the sitz baths, the ice bag, the
light treatments—to be an adequate bonding force with
other women. Standing in our robes in front of the nursery window looking at our newborns, we sense our kin-
ship. We unabashedly compare birth weights, labor stories, and our other children's reactions to the birth. There
is a brief moratorium on competitiveness. Questions about
who we are apart from our motherhood are irrelevant for

these few days. During visiting hours at the window, my husband has to endure the predictable remark, "Starting your own basketball team, huh?" from the backslapping Fabergé salesman who has just had his third girl—"Well, yes, we've got a regular little Brownie troop now."

If I had any anxieties about having this third child, the media came to my rescue. Shortly after I learned I was pregnant, *Harper's* magazine made me feel absolutely noble with its cover story, "The Family out of Favor," by Michael Novak. "The courage to marry and raise children presupposes a willingness to grow up," Novak writes. "To choose to have a family used to be interesting. It is, today, an act of intelligence and courage." John and I had made a political statement and didn't even know it. Several weeks after I came home from the hospital, *New York* magazine dotted its cover with babies and forecast that by 1980 pregnancy would be chic. Courageous and chic, too? No wonder my childless friends who used to take impulse trips to Zihuatenejo are now looking for a house in the "right" school district. What the magazines forgot to say, however, is that tiny babies are delicious, moist little bundles of unknown promise; that they are very warm on a cold night; that they have piercing, omniscient stares while feeding and irresistible absurd grins when satisfied; that their needs in these early weeks, especially when compared with the needs of six- and four-year-old sons and the other bewildering demands on our lives, are so pleasantly uncomplicated. Welcome, little William. It took three for me to notice.

A Christmas Diary

I PUT AWAY Christmas cards today and paused to look wistfully at my cousin Lynn's greeting—a photograph of her young daughters, standing under a Christmas wreath. They were wearing long red dresses with white pinafores and carrying red candles. How different her Christmas experiences must be—not because she lives in Little Rock and I live in Dallas, but because she has three daughters and I have three sons.

Little girls, I think, must look at Christmas with a sense of wonder and say, "How pretty." The little boys I know snatch their Christmas, shake it, lick it, turn it upside down, and then ask, "What does it do?"

Each Christmas, try as I might to orchestrate tradition, graciousness, and grateful hearts, these small boys never fail to inject some variable that knocks my holiday scenario askew. William is only four weeks old this Christmas, but I can tell by the way he grins when his brothers say, "Way to go, William—that was a neato burp!" that by next December he'll be in their camp, merrily trouncing my Christmas fantasies.

Here's how it happened this year.

December 10. The stockings were hung today. And

rehung. And then there was a fight about the position of the stockings. Jack, the six-year-old, won. The small wooden crèche is now assembled, or disassembled, depending on whether you believe, as does Drew, that all the beasts, angels, shepherds, Wise Men, and Holy Family huddled hoof to elbow under the roof of that stable or you align yourself with my other medieval scholar, who says, "Some of them stayed out in the yard, stupid." Another fight; Mary and a shepherd under the couch.

December 11. Jack came home from school with a note saying he must have a choirboy costume for the school play by December 15. And I have to make it. I desperately look over my shoulder for the real mother to take charge. The amount of sewing I've done since I married would scarcely use up one spool of thread. Thinking perhaps I can "wing it" with safety pins and pinking shears, I call a mother of daughters down the street to borrow her shears.

I ask her how Christmas is coming along at their house. "Well, the girls had their little friends over to ice the cookies yesterday. And this year we're decorating T-shirts with acrylic paint for their friends." (Just thinking of my sons' friends and acrylic paint makes me shudder.) She continues: "Last year we did lollipop cookies, using popsicle sticks, and tied them with gingham bows. We also go caroling. And the girls have decorated their rooms with herald angels cut out of cardboard and covered with gingham, and the bread-dough ornaments we made for their little tree."

A mother of sons goes through contortions to protect edible decorations. Another mother of sons down the block admitted to me that she almost broke her wrist fending off her sons from a fragile Santa with an apothecary jar of candy canes in his arms. And of twenty intricately sculptured sugar-plum ornaments sent by a well-meaning grandmother, only three remain. "And they have teeth marks," she says.

December 12. Today a good friend brought the boys Advent calendars, the kind with small doors to be opened each day until Christmas. The boys have two such calendars, but we don't refuse these because there has already been some cheating on the first ones. "Jack says he already knows what's behind my number twenty-five," wails Drew. The anticipation of Christmas is very cruel for this four-year-old. He cried himself to sleep tonight, hiccuping and wailing, "Why isn't Christmas tomorrow?"

Even Jack became hysterical tonight when we decreed bedtime before the "Drummer Boy" television special was over. The story always makes him cry anyway. How is it that a child can muster such compassion for a puppet and then "cream" his own brother for knocking his toothbrush into the toilet?

December 13. Jack and Drew went with their dad to the Christmas-tree lot this afternoon. They returned, gleeful, with a beautiful tree and a most uncharitable story about how the man at the lot tried to "rip them off." Now anyone admiring our tree gets the full story of how the hostile world is out to get you.

December 15. The first-grade Christmas program is over, and as the mother of sons I found it reassuring to see that little girls, even those dressed in angel wings, also pick their noses on stage. It was a traditional pageant. A little boy named Eisenberg played Joseph; a mischievous Vietnamese child with black bangs wore the donkey costume and shepherds wearing soccer kneepads knelt solemnly before the manger. A lovely blond Star of Bethlehem sighed audibly and rose in the east, but her arms got tired long before the Wise Men arrived. The choir performed without a hitch, and we blinked back tears as we watched these very serious-faced six-year-olds lisp, "Haste, haste to bring him laud, the Babe, the Son of Mary."

December 21. Christmas cards continue to pour in. I feel guilty at having sent only five—and those, the postman assures me, will not arrive before the twenty-fifth. I flip through the photograph cards and wonder what sort of threats were used to achieve these spontaneous grins on the faces of my friends' children. It does my heart good to see that my more artistic friends who have remained in academia and who were, I thought, leading purer lives than ours, sent a card with their eight-year-old son giving the "Fonz Ay-ay-ay-ay."

December 22. It rained today and the boys indulged me all afternoon. We stayed in front of the fireplace and read my favorite Christmas stories. We lighted the candles on the spin-around-the-angel chime, lay on our backs to watch the shadows on the ceiling and listened to Dylan Thomas's recording of "A Child's Christmas in Wales."

I was a little disappointed that the soccer ball landed in my poinsettia, but on the whole the afternoon came closer to my Christmas card fantasies than anything else to date.

December 24. The longest day of the year for these little boys. I am relieved that grandparents who are willing to lose eternally at checkers, dominoes, and Go Fish have come to town.

Christmas Eve dinner will not be particularly elaborate this year, and fortunately there are no toys to assemble. All my anxiety is focused on the five-o'clock Holy Communion service, when Jack will receive Communion for the first time. How meaningful is the experience going to be for a six-year-old who tells his soccer-playing buddies that he has to go to church this afternoon, where you get this junk (the Host) from this goofy guy (the priest)?

The church is beautiful with poinsettias filling the nave. I am a little envious of the poised mothers whom I see with their little daughters sitting so patiently in green velvet Christmas dresses. Those mothers cannot know the struggle I endure every time my boys have to wear Sunday clothes. Little girls do not habitually kick the kneeling benches, so their mothers are spared the ritual of removing shoes when seated in church.

I'll bet this calm, collected mother in front of me doesn't even have a stock of Lifesavers in her purse to be doled out as rewards at half time (the offertory). Or if she does, she doesn't worry that during the Agnus Dei someone will shout, "He always gets the red one."

Her daughter, who is in Jack's First Communion class, returns from the altar rail, kneels, and says in a stage whisper, "Thank you, Jesus, for the bread and wine." My son says, "You're welcome," giggles, and gets pinched.

Our turn comes, and when we return to our pew I notice that Jack has something concealed in his hand. The wafer? No, a small vial of medicine wrapped in gauze—smelling salts! "Found it while we were waiting around on our knees up there, and you can't have it," he whispers. As discreetly as possible, I try to wrest it from him while we sing "Silent Night." He clenches it firmly in his fist and I am sure that any further struggling will send it crashing to the slate floor, so I settle for "Don't you dare drop it" sung to the tune of "O Come, All Ye Faithful." He doesn't drop it; he puts it in his mouth and absentmindedly bites down on it. Shrieks, blood, glass and ammonia fumes spew from his mouth. We cannot stay for "O Come, O Come, Emmanuel."

Bedtime is never more difficult to enforce than on Christmas Eve. Tonight they stall with dozens of unanswerable theological questions and misconceptions.

"How do angels fly?"

"When was God born?"

"Boy, there must be a bunch of Jesuses now if we get a new one every Christmas."

"Do you think Papa's dog Siggi could just jump out of heaven into Santa's sleigh and be here in the morning?"

Drew is so exhausted that he forgets to say, "Yuk" when I kiss him good night. Jack protests, but when I lean close to his face, he blurts out painfully, "You know, there really isn't a Santa . . . He's just a spirit . . . I think." He pulls the pillow over his head to avoid my confirmation.

I never sleep on Christmas Eve. I'm not listening for Santa; I'm listening for little feet. I have a horror of having to begin Christmas Day at 2 A.M. Sure enough, Jack joins me for William's two-o'clock feeding. "My bed is too boring," he says.

When William is back in his crib, I offer my lap to this forty-eight-pound child. With no peers or brother to tease him, he snuggles willingly with me in the familiar rocking chair and insists that I make up new nonsense verses to "Go Tell Aunt Rhody."

His body is so squirmy with anticipation that even the rhythm of the rocking chair can't relax him. "I think he's been here, Mom," he says. "Can't I just go peek?"

We compromise. He can go back to bed and take his portable radio and earplugs.

December 25. After my sleepless night, wouldn't you know all three children would oversleep! I fix the coffee; John rigs up the movie camera, burning his hand on the light in the process; and when we can stand it no longer, we wake them up. They have forgotten what day it is and have to be led to the living room. I am so eager for them to see their new treasures that for once they seem to move in slow motion.

Jack rubs his eyes in disbelief when he sees his new bike. Drew seems genuinely thrilled with his brother's hand-me-down bike, shiny with its new Mickey Mouse bell attached. But before I know it, the tranquil moment of contentment is destroyed. Jack, with a snazzy new racing bike, is matter-of-factly stripping his brother's bike of handlebar grips, padded roll bar, and license plate. "You can have the bike, Drew," he says, "but not these." The tears begin.

The arrival of grandparents ameliorates this scene, and I suggest that Jack be our Santa Claus and deliver presents to the grown-ups, now that he has learned to read the tags.

He takes a dim view of my suggestion. "There's nothing left under that tree for me, so I'm going to my room."

So much for the spirit of giving.

I look at his loot as he begins to drag it back to his lair. My boys' godparents, also the parents of boys, sent Evel Knieval Stunt Circuses, battery-powered racing cars, and racetracks with plastic parts to be assembled with rubber bands.

Presents unwrapped, I bring out the Christmas coffee-cake. A friend drove forty miles to a German community to buy us this lovely bread with green and red cherries on top. "Oooh, gross," the boys moan. "Don't we have any Cheerios?"

What did I expect? They are very young and, as my husband constantly reminds me, they are boys. Forgive me, feminists, it makes a difference. They will never ask Santa to bring them handcrafted miniature furniture for an exquisite dollhouse. And they will always say, "Weird" when I finger red satin Mary Jane shoes with green embroidery on the toes in an antique shop. They will always prefer the part in Dylan Thomas's "A Child's Christmas in Wales" where the boys snowball the cats to the part about bells that ring inside you.

January 6. Christmas isn't entirely over. There is still the church Epiphany pageant. I am the "Virgin Mary," and I have not been chosen for my natural radiance; I have the part because Baby William is too young to be trusted with a fresh-faced teenager. We sit in the nave of the church. The spotlight goes on us, and miraculously my tiny, moist son hams it up by smiling and tugging at my Madonna scarf. "And lo, there were shepherds abiding in the field. . . ." Four-year-old Drew plays a shepherd, costumed in his dirty sneakers and his Batman bathrobe worn wrong side out. He kneels at the manger and challenges my composure by holding his nose and saying "Peeeeeeeeyew" at the baby in my arms.

When the costumes are put away for another year and we are riding home from the church, Drew asks, "Why don't we ever have a real Christmas?"

"What do you think I've been trying to do?" I say.

"No, I mean a real Christmas—you know, we could get some hay and a bunch of cows and donkeys. . . ."

I like to remember that the Virgin Mary was not the mother of daughters either.

Masculine/Feminine

I HAD EVERY intention to raise liberated, nonviolent sons whose aggressive tendencies would be mollified by a sensitivity and compassion that psychologists claim were denied their father's generation.

I did not buy guns or war toys (although Grandmother did). My boys even had a secondhand baby doll until the garage sale last summer. I did buy Marlo Thomas's *Free to Be You and Me* record, a collection of nonsexist songs, stories, and poems, and I told them time and time again that it was okay to cry and be scared sometimes. I overruled their father and insisted that first grade was much too early for organized competitive soccer leagues. They know that moms *and dads* do dishes and diapers. And although they use it primarily for the convenient bathroom between the alley and the sandpile, my boys know that the storeroom is now Mother's office. In such an environment, surely they would grow up free of sex-role stereotypes. At the very least wouldn't they pick up their own socks?

My friends with daughters were even more zealous. They named their daughters strong, cool unisex names like Blakeney, Brett, Brook, Lindsay, and Blair, names that lent themselves to corporate letterheads, not Tupperware party invitations. These moms looked on Barbie with disdain and bought trucks and science kits. They shunned frilly dresses for overalls. They subscribed to Feminist Press and read stories called "My Mother the Mail Carrier" instead of "Sleeping Beauty." At the swimming pool one afternoon, I watched a particularly fervent young mother, ironically clad in a string bikini, encourage her daughter, "You're so strong, Blake! Kick hard, so you'll be the strongest kid in this pool." When my boys splashed water in Blakey's eyes and she ran whimpering to her mother, this mom exhorted, "You go back in that pool and shake your fist like this and say, 'You do that again and I'll bust your lights out.'" A new generation of little girls, assertive and ambitious, taking a backseat to no one?

It's a little early to assess the results of our efforts, but when Jack comes home singing—to the tune of "Frère Jacques"—"Farrah Fawcett, Farrah Fawcett, I love you" and five minutes later asks Drew if he'd like his nose to be a blood fountain, either we're backsliding or there's more to this sex-role learning than the home environment can handle.

I'm hearing similar laments from mothers of daughters. "She used to tell everyone that she was going to grow up to be a lawyer just like Daddy," said one, "but she's hedging on that ambition ever since she learned that no one wears a blue fairy tutu in the courtroom." Another mother with two sons, a daughter, and a very successful career notes that, with no special encouragement, only her daughter keeps her room neat and loves to set the table and ceremoniously seat her parents. At a Little League game during the summer, fearful that this same young daughter might be absorbing the stereotype "boys play

while girls watch," her parents readily assured her that
she too could participate when she was eight years old.
"Oh," she exclaimed with obvious delight, "I didn't know
they had cheerleaders."

How does it happen? I have my own theories, but decided to do a little reading to see if any of the "experts"
agreed with me. I was also curious to find out what
remedies they recommended. The books I read propose
that sex roles are culturally induced. In simplistic terms,
rid the schools, their friends, and the television of sexism,
and your daughters will dump their dolls and head
straight for the boardroom while your sons contemplate
nursing careers. *Undoing Sex Stereotypes* by Marcia Guttentag and Helen Bray is an interesting study of efforts to
overcome sexism in the classroom. After reading it, I
visited my son's very traditional school and found it
guilty of unabashedly perpetrating the myths that feminists abhor. Remember separate water fountains? And
how, even if the line was shorter, no boy would be caught
dead drinking from the girls' fountain and vice versa?
That still happens. "You wouldn't want me to get cooties,
would you, Mom?" my son says, defending the practice.
What did I expect in a school where the principal still
addresses his faculty, who range in age from twenty-three
to seventy-five, as "girls"?

Nevertheless, having been a schoolteacher myself, I am
skeptical of neatly programmed nonsexist curriculum
packets like Guttentag and Brays. But if you can wade
through the jargon ("people of the opposite sex hereafter
referred to as POTOS"), some of the observations and ex-
ercises are certainly thought-provoking and revealing. In
one exercise fifth-grade students were asked to list adjectives appropriate to describe women. The struggle some
of the children had in shifting their attitudes about tradi-

tional male roles is illustrated in this paragraph written by a fifth-grade girl who was asked to write a story about a man using the adjectives she had listed to describe women:

> Once there was a boy who all his life was very *gentle*. He never hit anyone or started a fight and when some of his friends were not feeling well, he was *loving* and *kind* to them. When he got older he never changed. People started not liking him because he was *weak, petite,* and he wasn't like any of the other men—not strong or tough. Most of his life he sat alone thinking about why no one liked him. He joined a baseball team, but he was no good, he always got out. Then he decided to join the hockey team. He couldn't play good. He kept on breaking all the rules. So he quit the team and joined the soccer team. These men were *understanding* to him. He was really good at soccer, and was the best on the team. That year they won the championship and the rest of his life he was happy.°

After reading this paragraph it occurred to me that this little girl's self-esteem and subsequent role in life would be enhanced by a teacher who spent less time on "non-sexist intervention projects" and more time on writing skills. But that, of course, is not what the study was meant to reveal.

The junior high curriculum suggested by *Undoing Sex Stereotypes* has some laudable consciousness-raising goals. For example, in teaching units called "Women's Role in American History" and "The Socialization of Women and the Image of Women in the Media," teenagers are en-

° From *Undoing Sex Stereotypes,* by Marcia Guttentag and Helen Bray, © 1976 McGraw-Hill, Inc. Used with permission of McGraw-Hill Book Co.

couraged to critically examine television commercials, soap operas, and comic books. But am I a traitor to the cause if I object when the authors in another unit use *Romeo and Juliet* as a study of the status of women? Something is rotten in Verona when we have to consider Juliet's career possibilities and her problems with self-actualization. The conclusions of this project were lost on me; I quit reading when the author began to talk about ninth-graders who were "cognitively at a formal-operational level." I don't even know what my "external socio-psychological situation" is. However, I think I did understand some of the conclusions reached by the kids:

"Girls are smart."

"If a woman ran a forklift where my father works, there would be a walkout."

"Men cannot be pom-pom girls."

Eminently more readable, considering that both authors are educators of educators, is *How to Raise Independent and Professionally Successful Daughters*, by Drs. Rita and Kenneth Dunn. The underlying and, I think, questionable assumption in this book is that little boys have been reared correctly all along. Without direct parental intervention, according to the Dunns, daughters tend to absorb and reflect society's values. The Dunns paint a dark picture indeed for the parents who fail to channel their daughters toward professional success. The woman who remains at home with children while her husband is involved in the "real world" with an "absorbing and demanding day-to-day commitment that brings him into contact with new ideas, jobs and people (attractive self-actualized females)" is sure to experience lowered IQ, according to the Dunns. They go on to predict the husband's inevitable affair and the subsequent divorce, which leaves the wife emotionally depressed and probably financially dependent on her parents.

Now I'm all for women developing competency and self-reliance, but the Dunns' glorification of the professional is excessive. Anyone who has worked longer than a year knows that eventually any job loses most of its glamour. And the world is no less "real" at home. For that matter, mothers at home may be more "real" than bankers or lawyers. How is a corporate tax problem more real than my counseling with the maid, whose boy friend shot her in the leg? How can reading a balance sheet compare with comforting a five-year-old who holds his limp cat and wants to know why we have to lose the things we love? And on the contrary, it is my husband, the professional, who complains of lowered IQ. Though we wooed to Faulkner, my former ace English major husband, now turned trial lawyer, has time for only an occasional *Falconer* or Peter Benchley thriller. Certainly there is value in raising daughters to be financially self-supporting, but there is not much wisdom in teaching a daughter that she must achieve professional success or her marriage probably won't last.

In a chapter called "What to Do from Birth to Two," the authors instruct parents to introduce dolls only if they represent adult figures or groups of figures. "Try not to give her her own 'baby.' A baby doll is acceptable only for dramatizing the familiar episodes she has actually experienced, like a visit to the doctor." If some unthinking person should give your daughter a baby doll, and she likes it, the Dunns recommend that you permit her to keep it without exhibiting any negative feelings, "but do not lapse into cuddling it or encouraging her to do so. Treat it as any other object and direct attention to other more beneficial toys." I wonder if the Dunns read an article by Anne Roiphe called "Can You Have Everything and Still Want Babies?" which appeared in *Vogue* a couple of years ago. Ms. Roiphe was deploring the extremes to which our liberation has brought us. "It is nice to have beautiful feet, it may be desirable to have small feet, but it is painful and abusive to bind feet. It is a good thing for women to have independence, freedom and choice, movement, and opportunity; but I'm not so sure that the current push against mothering will not be another kind of binding of the soul. . . . As women we have thought so little of ourselves that when the troops came to liberate us we rushed into the streets leaving our most valuable attributes behind as if they belonged to the enemy."

The Dunns' book is thorough, taking parents step by step through the elementary years and on to high school. Had I been raising daughters, however, I think I would have flunked out in the chapter "What to Do from Age Two to Five." In discussing development of vocabulary, the Drs. Dunn prohibit the use of nonsensical words for bodily functions. I'm sorry, Doctors, but I've experimented with this precise terminology and discovered that the child who yells "I have to defecate, Mom" across four grocery aisles is likely to be left in the store. A family without a few poo-poo jokes is no family at all.

These educators don't help me much in my efforts to liberate my sons. And although I think little girls are getting a better deal with better athletic training and broader options, I believe we're kidding ourselves if we think we can raise our sons and daughters alike. Certain inborn traits seem to be immune to parental and cultural tampering. How can I explain why a little girl baby sits on a quilt in the park thoughtfully examining a blade of grass, while my baby William uproots grass by handfuls and eats it? Why does a mother of very bright and sensitive daughters confide that until she went camping with another family of boys, she feared that my sons had a hyperactivity problem? I'm sure there are plenty of rowdy, noisy little girls, but I'm not just talking about rowdiness and noise. I'm talking about some sort of primal physicalness that causes the walls of my house to pulsate on rainy days. I'm talking about something inexplicable that makes my sons fall into a mad, scrambling, pull-your-ears-off-kick-your-teeth-in heap just before bedtime, when they're not even mad at each other. I mean something that causes them to climb the doorjamb with honey and peanut butter on their hands while giving me a synopsis of *Star Wars* that contains only five intelligible words: "And then this guy, he 'psshhhhhhh.' And then this thing went 'Vrongggggg.' But this little guy said, 'Nonh-neeee-nonh-neee.'" When Jack and Drew are not kicking a soccer ball or each other, they are kicking the chair legs, the cat, the baby's silver rattle, and, inadvertently, Baby William himself, whom they have affectionately dubbed "Tough Eddy." Staying put in a chair for the duration of a one-course meal is torturous for these boys. They compensate by never quite putting both feet under the table. They sit with one leg doubled under them while the other leg extends to one side. The upper half of the body appears committed to the task at hand—eating—but the lower extremities are poised to lunge should a more compelling distraction present itself. From this position, I have observed, one brother can trip a haughty dessert-eating sibling who is flaunting the fact that he ate all his "sweaty little peas." Although we have civilized them to the point that they dutifully mumble, "May I be excused, please?" their abrupt departure from the table invariably overturns at least one chair or whatever milk remains.

This sort of constant motion just doesn't lend itself to lessons in thoughtfulness and gentleness.

Despite my encouragement, my sons refuse to invite little girls to play anymore. Occasionally friends leave their small daughters with us while they run errands. I am always curious to see what these females will find of interest in my sons' roomful of Tonka trucks and soccer balls. One morning the boys suggested that the girls join them in playing emergency with the big red fire trucks and ambulance. The girls were delighted and immediately designated the ambulance as theirs. The point of emergency, as I have seen it played countless times with a gang of little boys, is to make as much noise with the siren as possible and to crash the trucks into each other or into the leg of a living-room chair before you reach your destination.

The girls had other ideas. I realized why they had selected the ambulance. It contained three dolls: a driver, a nurse, and a sick man on the stretcher. My boys have used that ambulance many times, but the dolls were always secondary to the death-defying race with the fire trucks; they were usually just thrown in the back of the van as an afterthought. The girls took the dolls out, stripped and redressed them tenderly, and made sure that they were seated in their appropriate places for the first rescue. Once the fire truck had been lifted off the man's leg, the girls required a box of Band-Aids and spent the next half hour making a bed for the patient and reassuring him that he was going to be all right. These little girls and my sons had seen the same NBC *Emergency* series, but the girls had apparently picked up on the show's nurturing aspects, while Jack and Drew were interested only in the equipment, the fast driving, and the sirens.

And what about the rerun of World War II that is being staged in our sandpile? I recently asked a friend, who has made every effort to raise her daughter to be free of sex-role stereotypes, what her daughter thought about war. "Laura's only mentioned it once that I can recall, and that was to abhor it and to want to be reassured that it was very far away from her home," she told me. My sons are lobbying to have the draft reinstated before their eighteenth birthdays. They have had minimal exposure to toy guns; they have seldom seen a war movie; and their father's army experience consisted of four months' active duty as a reservist driving a dump truck. I have accused him of grossly exaggerating for them the time he spent crawling under live machine-gun fire at Fort Leonard Wood, but, on the whole, he is a gentle person. Is it their penchant for action that predisposes them to pore over war toys in the Dinky catalog at rest time when I had hoped we could finish reading *Charlotte's Web?* They direct our dinner-table conversation toward the merits of Leopard tanks and antiaircraft missiles. Their father holds his own rather well, but I simply have no opinions when it comes to Stukas versus Spitfires. In this house where the chances of finding a toilet seat down are one to four, I sometimes feel like an alien. Last night both boys were in bed listening in the dark to Rosey Grier singing "It's all right to cry" from the album *Free to Be You and Me.* Seeing that Jack had buried his head in his pillow, I thought perhaps the record had triggered the recall of some sad moment of his day. I sat on the side of his bed, patted his shoulder and waited for the full confession. He turned over absolutely dry-eyed and asked, "Mom, do you think an M-16 bullet can blow up a tank?"

They were sent to SMU piano preparatory, not Fort Polk, so how do they know about these things? The eight-year-old girl next door, a bright, lively child who wears a baseball cap and walks on her hands as well as she walks on her feet, wandered into the backyard battlefield one afternoon and reluctantly agreed to a "short setup." From what I can observe, this involves lining up your plastic army men and tanks in trenches dug in the sandpile and positioning your radio men on the hills. Kelly, the young lady, lined her soldiers up admirably, but when she marched one to the top of the hill and said, "Pow!" the boys collapsed in uncontrollable giggles. "Pow? Kelly, is that what you said?" "Don't you know what an M-16 sounds like?" "Don't you know you could never expose a man like that without air cover?" Tears welled in her eyes as she bolted out of the yard to rejoin the rope skippers across the street. "I'm not playing with you anymore, Jack Mackintosh!" she yelled. "You don't play fair. Just because I said 'Pow' you won't admit that I've killed any of your stupid old army." I shared her humiliation. I too had flunked a short setup earlier in the summer. I have yet to meet a female who can make, or is even interested in making, the various noises that indicate the progress of an air raid. I'm glad; it makes the neighborhood about 50 per cent quieter than it would be otherwise.

Someone asked me if William, my number three son, had been a daughter would I have treated her any differently? Of course I would. As one perceptive friend remarked, "Sex identity is all a baby can tell you at first, and of course you're going to respond to it." Most little girls seem to come equipped with a sense of wonder that I can only hope my sons will acquire with maturity. As for now, if Jack and Drew can't snatch it, shake it, lick it, or turn it upside down and jump on it, they don't like it. This attitude seriously inhibits our sunset watching, stargazing, and introspective character-building conversations. Lapsing into what my husband cynically calls my "beauty of the theory" child-rearing mood, I once planned a family outing to Old City Park in Dallas. Surely the boys would enjoy a picnic in the park with an oompah band in the gazebo, real lemonade, and people in turn-of-the-century costumes. "This will really be fun," I told them. "You'll get to see a real log cabin and toys like the ones your great-grandpa Porter might have played with. You might see a general store like the one you've seen on 'The Waltons,' and I'll even let you have your picture made in funny old-fashioned clothes." They were quiet when I finished my sales pitch. Then Jack spoke up: "I'll tell you what, Mom. We'll go on one condition." "What's that?" I asked. "Only if they have pinball machines."

My sons' attitudes toward women are difficult to measure at this point in their lives. They are willing to grant girls equality and even superiority in intellectual realms. "Christy and Mary Ellen have bionics in their heads," Jack says. "They were just born knowing how to read." He is convinced that he will never be able to equal female scholastic performance even when he receives a letter from one of the wonder women that says, "I lick you, Jack. Love, Jenny." He, of course, still writes birthday cards that say, "To Jenny, Form Jack."

"I don't like any girls," I overheard Jack say to one of his buddies, "except my mom." While I am flattered to have made the cut, being the primary female role model for three boys sometimes makes me a little self-conscious. What about a mom who cries and can't throw a ball straight? While we may be morally committed to feminism as an issue, I suspect a lot of us who experienced some successes under the old rules may be waffling in our daily behavior. My sons view everything I do with such utter objectivity that I am continually having to account for the idiosyncrasies of my sex. Explaining pregnancy and childbirth is almost minor once you've tackled the really difficult subjects like leg shaving and eyebrow plucking. They were speechless the day they caught me with bleach cream slathered on my upper lip. "I know you think this is ridiculous," I said nervously, "but you wouldn't like it if your mother was mistaken for Errol Flynn."

Of course, I want my sons to grow up knowing that what's inside a woman's head is more important than her appearance, but I'm sure they're getting mixed signals when I delay our departure for the swimming pool to put on lipstick. I also wonder what they make of their father, whose favorite aphorism is "Beautiful women rule the world." I suppose what we want for these sons and the women they may marry someday is a sensitivity that enables them to be both flexible and at ease with their respective roles so that marriage contracts and Marabel Morgan are unnecessary. When my sons bring me the heads of two purple irises from the neighbor's yard and ask, "Are you really the most beautiful mama in the whole world like Daddy says, and did everyone want to marry you?" do you blame me if I keep on waffling?

Love Thy Neighborhood

WE ARE SELLING our house and moving. Baby William is eighteen months old, and his days in the high chair are numbered; with no room at the table for him, so are the days in our first home. The house that was adequate for two sons has somehow become claustrophobic with three. Nevertheless, the for-sale sign in our front yard makes us a little uneasy, because the realtor's ad in the Sunday paper—"cute, spacious, airy Tudor"—ignores the thing we hate to lose most. This cute Tudor with the heights of three little boys marked inside a closet door and a *Star Wars* poster glued to one wall comes with a neighborhood.

For seven years we have lived in this pre-World War II suburb. Many of the houses are built with porches, there are sidewalks, and the neighborhood was originally zoned to permit stores within walking distance. Modest places like ours are interspersed with grander remodeled two-story houses. A half dozen new houses suggest that this is a neighborhood in transition, but changes come slowly here, or at least they used to. In fact, I still identify my house as the Dyers' house. They lived here for nearly forty years, and I like the fact that little boys who are now grown men once painted Keep Out on one wall of our garage and embedded their BBs in the other. Two of my sons are immortalized by names, dates, and handprints in the alley, which was paved only three years ago.

Our neighborhood schools are a strong unifying force. Our children walk to school together. The crossing guard at the busy intersection not only knows them by name but also chides them for sleeping late and reminds them that their library books are probably overdue. Children don't come home for lunch anymore, so volunteering mothers operate the cafeteria at the school.

Seven years ago we gave little thought to the neighborhood; we simply liked the house and we could just about afford it. But if we took little notice of the neighborhood, the neighborhood did not ignore us. Another newcomer to the block with two small children called shortly after we were settled. While we drank our tea, our children set about at once establishing their pecking order. Jack, my then amiable toddler, emerged scratched and bleeding from his first encounter with the neighborhood girls. I emerged with the confidence of having a close neighbor who had recently lived through toilet training. A mother of three eventually leased the duplex at the opposite end of the street, and the three of us spent many a late afternoon sitting on my porch or their front steps watching the tricycle traffic of our offspring. Although frequently interrupted by a dirty diaper, a skinned knee, a runny nose, or a temporarily broken heart, we idly exchanged information about pediatricians, kids' eating habits, earaches, first-grade teachers, swimming lessons, babysitters, and, of course, peculiar neighbors. These were the sorts of conversations that we might have frowned upon had we not been mothers who desperately needed to overcome the isolation of dealing with small children all day. Here we could admit without embarrassment or guilt that we had hurled an entire jar of grape jelly against the wall when we found a purple-smeared baby eating jelly amid the freshly folded laundry.

We didn't think those hours were very important at the time, but when I talk with my friends with careers who waited until their thirties to start families, I realize that they have missed that easy reassurance and folk wisdom that come from daily association with similarly occupied women. Their homes are frequently the lovely but isolated houses afforded by two salaries. The view is beautiful, but there's no place to roller-skate. Without other neighborhood moms, they must rely on their pediatricians or often their maids for the comforting knowledge that colicky screamers *will* eventually sleep through the night, or that a baby who is not bathed promptly at ten o'clock in the morning won't contract scabies by nightfall.

Another mother in the next block with less time or inclination to share our afternoon reflections, primarily because she was so darn good at being the mother of five children, also came to welcome me to the neighborhood. I really can't remember Nancy ever coming to my door empty-handed. This first time she brought cookies for my toddler and an African violet started from a cutting the former owner of my house had given her. Never have I met a more skilled mother, nor have I in recent years met one so totally fulfilled by her chosen domestic role. A woman of seemingly indefatigable energies, she baked bread regularly, filled her freezer with fancy cupcakes, sewed her daughters' clothes, slipcovered her furniture, gave her sons haircuts, and kept a greenhouse and a huge dog thriving. She never forgot the little-old-lady neighbors or her children's schoolteachers, or Ray, the safety patrolman, on their respective birthdays, and she spent her free time wearing a clown costume to entertain crippled children at Scottish Rite Hospital. When she moved away in 1975, I realized that she was the stuff of which good neighborhoods are made and that her species is endangered.

With Nancy gone, the next best attraction in our neighborhood from the children's point of view is Don, the bachelor airline pilot. Because of his flying schedule, he is often home during the day and consequently does more unpaid babysitting than anyone else on the block. At Don's house, my sons tell me, you can help him work on his Ferraris, dial the Budweiser Song number as often as you want, eat salami out of the refrigerator, watch what Mother calls "junk" on television, and sometimes go get a Slurpee without hearing what it does to your teeth. With his aerodynamic skills, he can keep kites airborne. Hardly an evening in the summer passes without at least six children lining up in his front yard to wait their turn doing acrobatics with Don, which they've named the "elevator" and the "airplane." He also teaches neat magic tricks, like how to take your thumb off and how to break your nose. I have been told he has in his house a laughing machine, a cuckoo clock, and maybe a slot machine. Endearing nicknames from mothers are greeted with a grimace, but Don can label Drew the Kangaroo and Jack the Rabbit with impunity.

The neighbors who live in this three-block expanse are people of diverse ages and interests, not best friends necessarily, but people who nevertheless have maintained a certain tenuous bond. Things used to be chummier than they are now, according to older neighbors. Ten or fifteen years ago, everyone on the block knew when and where you were going on your vacation. As your car pulled away, neighbors sometimes stuffed small treats for the children or surprise "survival" kits in the car windows. At the very least they stood in their front yards and waved good-bye. While you treated your sunburn in Galveston, you could be sure that the neighbors were not only faithfully watching your house but also mowing and watering your St. Augustine. Frequently a welcome-home banner with a supper invitation would be strung across your house on your return. Throughout the year the whole block celebrated children's birthdays. Shortly before we moved here, a neighborhood son returned from Vietnam and the street was roped off for a block party in his honor.

These same thoughtful people gave a morning coffee to welcome us newcomers to the neighborhood seven years ago. Since then I have attended wedding showers for girls who grew up on this block, my children have participated in Easter-egg hunts, and when Poppy, a popular neighborhood grandfather who has been known to fire off a shotgun to welcome the New Year, turned eighty, a rented billboard invited all of us—from octogenarians to toddlers—to celebrate. Entire meals from neighbors appeared each time I returned from the hospital with my babies. A death elicits similar responses. The longest day of the year for our children, Christmas Eve, is made more endurable by the yearly appearance of Mr. Brown, a high school math teacher, who delivers his wife's homemade gingerbread men to each child. Newcomers to our block are soon treated to dinner at the home of the retired neighbors, who have lived here the longest. They have no air conditioning, no television, and no automobile and never have. Because their windows are open much of the year and because they walk everywhere—to the supermarket, to church, to plays and concerts at the nearby university—they are an excellent source of news about the neighborhood. Somehow I think my generation is less prone to sustain these small traditions that give cohesion to such an unlikely mix of folks. The Fourth of July parade is a case in point.

For more than twenty years the three blocks have joined together to celebrate the Fourth of July with a parade. The children decorate their tricycles, bikes, and Big Wheels. A fire engine and police car from our suburban departments and a Boy Scout color guard lead the procession. A neighbor who has a farm sometimes brings her horses in for the occasion. Another neighbor, a federal judge, leads us in the Pledge of Allegiance, and someone delivers a brief patriotic stump speech. Once a visiting opera singer sang "The Star-Spangled Banner." After the parade, cookies and lemonade made by volunteers complete the ritual by midmorning. If it sounds a little corny, it is; but for a variety of reasons, it is the only occasion that gets us all out together anymore. Even this remaining tradition, with more and more people on vacations in Colorado or with the kids in camp for four weeks, becomes progressively less elaborate every year. And last year we almost lost it altogether when the who-to-call-to-get-the-parade-together book and the flag passed along by the previous coordinator somehow got misplaced until the last minute. That would never have happened ten years ago, and it was just another small sign of the creeping suburbanization that appears to be taking over. Changes that have occurred in our few blocks in the past decade may have upgraded our property values, but ironically they have contributed to increasing isolation. There is no doubt that we are becoming a more affluent neighborhood, and with that affluence we tend to buy our privacy, not neighborhood togetherness.

Even in our own house, the changes are apparent. Two

years after we moved in, we had central heat and air conditioning installed. As the cost of heating and cooling has climbed, we are less likely to leave the kitchen door open. No one drops in without calling anymore. That same year we also enclosed the side porch. We needed the extra room and gave little thought to the role that porches play in binding neighborhoods. Neighbors who wouldn't think of knocking on your front door for an informal visit can see you on a porch and not feel that they are imposing. Similarly, fenced backyards are becoming almost compulsory. But no matter how well equipped an enclosed yard may be, if it blocks the rest of the neighborhood from view, children won't play in it for long. Nothing beats the spontaneity of coming and going out front. Big Wheels and bikes make way for briskly striding heart patients, joggers, and dog walkers. Frisbees can be thrown across two lawns. Locked in their own backyard, little boys might miss the adolescent mechanics with their Mopeds and the chance to retch and gag when the teenage girl across the street kisses her boy friend good-bye after school.

Besides the fences, sprinkler systems and hired yardmen have appeared on the block. Neighbors spend less time in the yard exchanging information about grubworms. In fact, more and more services that were provided within the neighborhood are now being done by specialists. Where we once kept each other's children, we now usually hire babysitters. Our appliances and televisions that once could be repaired by a neighbor with mechanical skills now require factory components not available at the nearby hardware store. Plant specialists make house calls, and I frequently see ads in the local paper for house sitters who feed your pets and take care of your mail and newspapers. Neighbors used to meet these needs. In the best of neighborhoods, there is still a delicately balanced relationship based on a faith in reciprocity. If I help you dig a stump out of your backyard, in time you will bring me soup when I'm sick. Those who understand the system know that to repay the favor too quickly is to offend the spirit in which it is done. If we volunteer to keep each other's kids, we must not keep score. Because the children have played at my house twice this week does not mean that they must play at yours twice next week. Babysitter co-ops are not the same as neighbors.

Young mothers entering the work force and older people moving to retirement communities or nursing homes are two more threats to neighborhood survival. Without neighbors at home during the day, children do not have the beneficial scrutiny of other adults. Hired babysitters and maids in other houses will not yell at my son if he runs the stop sign on the corner. They don't know his name: my neighbors do. Without a neighbor, how would I know that out of my earshot Jack was calling his younger brother a vulgar name clearly unacceptable at home?

From my own working experience, I know that working mothers are more selfish with their time. In the four years that elapsed between my second and third sons, those aimless but valuable hours that women used to spend with other mothers seem to have disappeared. Either my organizational abilities have diminished or the pace of life has greatly accelerated in that brief span of time. Of the three mothers who sat on my porch when my second son was a baby, one is divorced, one has moved to the West Coast, and I now spend Tuesdays and Thursdays at the typewriter. Who has the time for a coffee klatch or even to push a baby stroller around the block?

Everybody seems to be spending his leisure time, if any, jogging alone.

Without thinking and because we can afford it, we complicate our lives unnecessarily. Children go to private preschools as soon as they are potty-trained, and our calendars fill up with car pooling, room mothering, Parents' Discovery Nights, and teacher conferences before the child has ever entered kindergarten. Hardly anyone learns to stand on his head or turn a somersault in the front yard; we drive them to the Y for gymnastics. Organized soccer leagues appear for five-year-olds. Whatever happened to jacks and hopscotch? Instead of telling stories on our front porch after dinner, we car-pool to the library at ten on Thursdays for story hour. Paints and clay are too messy for our recently remodeled homes, so we arrange for art lessons at the museum. Music teachers in my childhood were the neighborhood eccentrics who always lived conveniently near the school or home. Now the children are driven to the local university for group lessons. I am told that the children in my neighborhood used to put on shows for the neighbors; I think our kids who have seen so much slickly packaged entertainment no longer trust their own ingenuity. As Jack, our eight-year-old, says, "Why would anybody want to watch us do anything, Mom, when they could just go see *Star Wars* again?"

Hand in hand with increasing property values in prosperous neighborhoods will come increasing homogeneity. Schoolteachers, journalists, and other middle-income folk can no longer afford to buy homes here. When everyone on the block is a doctor, lawyer, or banker, the pool of talents we could share and the variety of skills we have to trade are diminished. When everyone's father and mother goes to work at an office somewhere downtown, children have fewer opportunities to see adults they know well doing meaningful work. "Sterilized suburbia . . . a strange period when every American wanted to become a mass-produced country squire," is the way Jean Briggs describes it in a recent issue of *Forbes*. "A whole generation has forgotten the pleasure of being able to walk to the nearest grocery store. To walk to work. They have become sadly accustomed to the back-breaking expense of keeping two or even three cars. And they are beginning to listen to psychologists who question whether suburbanities are really doing their children a favor by raising them in antiseptic, homogeneous communities."

As a matter of fact, the year after we moved here, O'Bannon's, a neighborhood store one block away, was razed to make way for look-alike town houses. With this zoning change, we not only lost the personal attention indigenous to mom-and-pop stores like O'Bannon's, but we also lost the convenience and possible educational advantages of dispatching young children to make midweek purchases of milk and bread. The only money dealings my children seem to have these days are with vending machines.

In spite of these changes, my sons still find plenty to love about this neighborhood, and they do not value all the emerging signs of affluence in their territory. The sprawling new house recently built near us was "okay" when it was still in the building stages, but now that it's finished, my eight-year-old surveys the carefully sodded lawn and asks, "Why did Mr. Jordan wanna go and wreck up that perfectly good vacant lot? He could've at least left one of those big sandpiles." In the eyes of an eight-year-old, a $300,000 house does nothing to enhance his turf.

What does enhance it is a fruit-bearing mulberry tree

across the street in the front yard of a rent house. This tree, which has been home base for at least two generations of after-supper hide-and-seek players, has limbs low enough for a five-year-old to climb. The fruit on the tree is good for stomping on the sidewalk, chunking, and indelibly staining your clothes. I am told that other ammunition called spear grass grows in our alley. We may have to take a cutting to the new neighborhood. Another natural phenomenon—and, according to my sons, a great selling point for our house—is the "worm farm," a low place in the street near our corner curb where mud and water collect to create an earthworm haven, good for fishing bait or just poking with a stick when your big brother and his friends have deserted you. Because we live only a block from the junior high school, there is no more lucrative corner than ours for a lemonade stand at four o'clock. This location also provides the possibility of some "big guy" dropping a contraband copy of *Mad* magazine in our yard on the way home from school.

In an article called "The Origins of Alienation," which appeared in *Scientific American* several years ago, and which I found full of sobering insights, Urie Bronfenbrenner cites the breakdown of neighborhoods as one of the prime factors in the increasing alienation of children and adults. (Other factors he mentions include the fragmentation of the extended family, the separation of residential and business areas, occupational mobility, supermarkets, television, separate patterns of social life for different age groups, the working mother, and the delegation of child care to specialists.) He notes that studies now show that children growing up in model communities with shaded walks, lawns, and fenced play areas feel isolated, regimented, and bored. "The study found that children gauged their freedom not by the extent of open areas around them but by the liberty they had to be among people and things that excited them and fired their imagination." Bronfenbrenner exhorts public and private planners to give consideration to the kind of world being created for the children who will grow up in new communities. He concludes with the proposal for nothing more radical than providing a setting in which young and old can simply sit and talk. "The fact that such settings are disappearing and have to be recreated deliberately," Bronfenbrenner says, "points both to the roots of the problem and to its remedy."

I sat last night on a neighbor's side porch, one of the few left in the neighborhood, hearing the thirty-year history of this block we've shared for only seven. She recalls days when every woman on the block swept her front walk daily and leaned on her broom for a neighborly chat. She blames television for keeping the neighbors isolated in their houses. Our local police chief blames air conditioning. "A power failure about eight or ten years ago in our area got some of the neighbors reacquainted one Sunday afternoon. It was real funny to see people back on the sidewalks and on their porches sitting and talking," he says. Maybe it's time for another one.

I am sometimes optimistic. There are still small signs here and there that suggest that our neighborhood is not irrevocably on its way to extinction and just may survive the Me Decade. The trading of neighborly skills may not be so much lost as changing in character. If I help the doctor in the next block write a speech for the Fourth of July parade, he might put a butterfly bandage on my accident-prone five-year-old. Hardly anyone of my generation in this neighborhood wields a screwdriver or a wrench with enough skill to offer assistance to anyone, but when a cardiologist we know who lives a couple of blocks away stops his jogging long enough to diagnose my lawyer husband's tension-related ills in exchange for a few malpractice war stories, I think we still have a neighborhood.

And obviously all ingenuity hasn't been stamped out of suburban children. Three enterprising eleven-year-old boys a few blocks away have published the *Belfort Banner* this summer. It is a hand-printed newspaper duplicated on the copier at someone's father's office and sold to the families on their block at subscription rates of six issues for a dollar. Regular features include a Guess Who column, which once described an editor's asthmatic little brother as "Guess who is very small and breaths like Darth Vader." The paper also provides puzzles, a few jokes, a cleanest-yard award, and something to color. (Several subscribers can't read yet.) Bringing old and young together, the small paper also permits an occasional mother's announcement like this one:

BULLETIN

The Wests' trampoline will be open to the public (that means you) from 6 to 10 at night when school is out. The summer hours are so we can sleep late and to preserve what little sanity poor Mrs. West has left. Don't bother knocking—just come on to the back gate.

We'll be moving to our new house this month. It's not so far away, and when I mentioned it to the police chief, he said, "Aw, northeast quadrant? They're real cozy over there." The "new" house is in fact another old one, where other little boys have jumped on the stairwell landing and caused a crack in the plaster. We will still have sidewalks and a larger porch than before. This time we won't enclose it.

Hoping Cio-Cio-San Will Die Before the Kickoff

I WAS NEVER a particularly feminine child growing up. At least I never thought of myself that way. I did play with dolls and perform dramatic ballet dances to radio music, but I also bit my fingernails, stepped on my untied sash, and was assigned the role of Cheeta the Chimp when my older brother and his gang played Tarzan of the Apes. Being a swarthy brunette in a hot climate, I still can't keep myself together the way cool blondes seem to do. I haven't been able to keep my hair out of my eyes since my mother stopped French braiding. But now that I live in a house with three young sons, a husband, and a tomcat, I'm trying harder. The need for a feminine influence is so painfully obvious around here; and it was clear that mine was inadequate the morning that Jack, my nine-year-old, asked, "Mom, have you ever had jock itch?"

With that impetus, I confess to recently stuffing my dresser drawers with sachet, having a manicure, and trimming crusts off a watercress sandwich for lunch more or less alone. William, now two years old, of course is still my constant luncheon partner. I am convinced that without some conscious attempts at feminine ritual around here, there is every possibility that we will all drown in a sea of mind-boggling physicalness, competitiveness, violence, and destruction.

This is my tale of violence and loveliness for all of the women who have said to me with ill-concealed envy, "It must be wonderful having all boys—being the queen of your household with no female rivals for their affection." The answer is "Yes . . . and no." Another mother of three sons put it this way: "You give up a lot."

Last year when I read John Irving's *The World According to Garp,* this line remained with me:

> She had a son of her own, after all, and she recognized the need of boys to devote themselves to a repetitious physical act. It seemed to relax them, Jenny had noticed, whether they were five or seventeen.

My sons have relaxed themselves by wagging brass hinges of antique lacquered boxes back and forth, by banging their heads together, and most recently by snapping the buttons on my intercom until the communication between my garage study and the house is permanently jammed. While I am cooking dinner, Drew practices mindless juggling with tennis balls until one lands in whatever is in the skillet on the range. Jack does baseball pitching windups during which he invariably forgets and sends a hardball flying into the pantry. Willie is content with rolling fruit off the end of the kitchen table.

Why would any mother permit that sort of behavior? Well, some of it starts so innocently. William was counting the apples before he started rolling them off the table. And I am not particularly attentive since I am trying in the midst of this perpetual motion to listen to my favorite

Public Radio news program while I stir the spaghetti sauce. The older boys are immediately repentant and seem as genuinely surprised as I am when something gets broken or splattered. Their own unconsciousness is their maddening defense.

I am a remarkably nonviolent, patient person. I have been refined in the fires of rush-hour traffic with irritable, thirsty children. However, three sons have also taught me the therapeutic value of screaming and sometimes throwing things. Other mothers will understand when I admit that I recently hit our nine-year-old with a plastic container full of leftovers. (Chinese food, which made it all the more effective.) Jack was badgering Drew about the way he set the table. Their relationship can be summed up in a brief sentence I found painstakingly engraved on a plastic place mat. "Drew is a domy and stencse." "Leave your brother alone," I yelled from the kitchen. "He's helping for once." Through the open door, I hear silverware hit the floor and the inevitable scuffling amid chair legs. That's when I hurled the leftover container which, quite honestly, I thought I had already emptied. It hit Jack squarely on the shoulder—chicken and slimy spinach. Childish behavior, I thought immediately. Horrible role model, of course. And cleaning up what landed on the floor and wall certainly was just penance. Nevertheless, I did get everyone's attention and dinner was conducted in relative peace.

I keep thinking that these sons will outgrow the need to be punching or kicking each other, but grown men have admitted to me that they still greet their brothers by frogging them in the arm or knuckling each other on the head. That's the hard part for a female to grasp. A lot of the head knocking and what I can only describe as jackass behavior is done with affection. My three, over my constant objection, have established a nighttime ritual before bed that involves tripping each other until someone cracks his head on a chair or bed and starts a wrestling match in earnest. I peer over my book and wonder why anyone would want to scramble on the floor and take a chance on getting a big toe jammed in his eye when he could brush his teeth and go to bed. My husband is a gentle man, but sometimes when I look to him to put a stop to it, I note that he is gritting his teeth on the verge of falling on the pile.

Nothing in my own childhood, not even the days I inflicted myself on my older brother's crowd, prepared me for the unrelenting competitiveness of my sons. Every minute of their day is spent comparing how fast, how far, how long, or how smart. "There!" Drew announces, slamming the milk cup down on the table. "I won the milk race." No contest, to my knowledge, had been announced. Jack dropped out of the Reading Club at the library last summer when he discovered it wasn't a race to see who could read the most books the fastest. Their premise seems to be "If it's not a contest, why do it?" They even imbue that most gentle of institutions, the library, with violent qualities. I overheard them filling out their library card applications. "Drew," Jack whispered, "you'll have to print that neater. The librarian will stomp your face in if you mess up another one of her cards."

Sometimes the destruction they wreak is merely a question of their taste versus mine. It never occurred to me that within twenty-four hours after we gained possession of our new/old house with its beautiful molding, stained glass, and beveled mirrors, the boys would have fouled it with Star Wars stick-ons. They reminded me of small dogs establishing their territory by lifting their legs in all corners. Drew found a piece of hot-pink chalk before the moving van even arrived and chalked his name (backward, of course) on the handsome masonry doorposts. Since the doorbell doesn't work, they still can't understand why I didn't like the blue-plastic Burger King door knocker they stuck to the front-door frame. The lovely walnut bannistered stairway which would seem to dictate a dignified descent has been used as a sledding chute for as many as five little boys on an air mattress. The arched front door with its twenty glass panes now has acrylite installed at William's knocking level. I have never been able to answer the door fast enough to suit him.

But these are the larger infringements that anyone visiting my house can observe. What you don't see are the smaller invasions of my sensibilities, the tiny desecrations of my personal possessions. Three examples will suffice. Thinking that at age thirty-five I could surely consider myself a grown-up lady, I treated myself to a nice fall handbag. I was practical enough to select cowhide because the saleslady promised that scratches and age would only give it character. I assured her that I needed something that could take the wear and tear. I dream someday of being the sort of lady whose purse is always organized with sunglasses in a case, makeup in a plastic lined case, small package of tissues, mending kit, nail file, and one nice gold pen kept in my balanced checkbook, but alas, the contents of my purse are a perpetual embarrassment. Today, it has:

six expired grocery coupons

a baseball needle

four pecans

two wrapped wads of chewed gum (Where did my sons get this fastidiousness about littering public places?)

Kleenex employed in a nosebleed in rush-hour traffic

an extra pair of training pants

a small wooden mallet (Some children carry security blankets; mine have always preferred hammers.)

a Lego spaceman we have dubbed "Mr. Bill"

an assortment of smeary ball-point or felt-tip pens

a small compact of grape-colored blusher which won't stay closed since someone knocked it to the floor while scrambling through my purse in search of lunch money

Just listing the mess makes me realize that I didn't deserve the handsome tobacco-colored bag. Such hubris did not go unpunished. Two days after I brought the bag home, a month before the bill for it arrived, I found William polka dotting one side of it with one of the felt-tip pens he had found on one of his gum-foraging missions. He was thoroughly enthralled with the way the ink spread when he touched the leather, and I'm sure he never understood why mommy stood in the doorway crying.

For years I have kept notebooks, diaries of a sort, sometimes notes for articles. As special incentive to write, I purchase blank bound books with beautiful paper that I find, appropriately, on the damaged merchandise table at the Horchow Collection outlet store. Never mind that the cover is a misprinted joke (*All I Knoow About Sex* or *Virtnous, Innocent, and Pure, My Story*) the paper is luxurious. But even these most private musings are violated. The flyleaf of my current notebook now bears the inscription "Luke, trust me" along with the obligatory laser-shooting spaceships.

The small Florentine box a friend sent me from Italy seven or eight years ago recently acquired a red-and-black decal that says something I don't even understand: "Hebdon Headers."

And then, of course, there are similar tramplings on the heart. Gifts and holidays are seldom accompanied by sentimentality. Oh, I have received my share of flower-head love offerings from grubby little fists, but more frequently little boys bring cicada shells. Mother's Day cards made in school art class are likely to remain in the backpacks if they make it home at all. Since the older boys had no money last Christmas to spend on gifts, I suggested that they make something for their little brother. I even provided a cozy work space in the attic so it would be a complete surprise for William. I suggested a felt puppet, a beanbag, or just a big picture especially drawn for him and provided all of the materials. They groaned at every suggestion and to my knowledge they never even went to the attic. Finally a few days before Christmas, I asked them how the project was coming. Jack took charge and said, "We've decided on what we're giving him and we'll just get it over with today." When Willie woke up from his nap, his older brothers took him into the kitchen, crammed two paper cups together, cut the bottom out of one, poured baking soda in it, then poured vinegar on the soda and called it a volcano. It did erupt all over the kitchen floor. "There you are, Willie," they said to the bewildered but delighted two-year-old, "that's your Christmas present."

I am convinced that if I did not make a point of inviting a guest, preferably a female guest or a grandmother to our Thanksgiving dinner, the china, the tablecloth, the silver would remain untouched. My sons, shirtless and barefoot (there is no "wild and blinding snow" in Texas on Thanksgiving) would be quite content to pick hunks of turkey off the stove, grimace at the giblet gravy, chase the corn bread with a swig of milk out of the plastic container in the refrigerator, and dash out the back door.

Recently at dinner one night when their father was out of town and we were eating early, I blew up about their allowing the cat to eat out of their plates at the table. Jack looked at me quite sympathetically and said, "Mom, I know this just drives you crazy, but we love him so much." The fact is, aside from the perfectly healthy gluttonous cat about whom they have cried innumerable times, they don't believe very much in feelings, yet. "Where are they?" my nine-year-old demands to know when I suggest that he has ignored mine. But, of course, he doesn't want to sit still for my explanation. Young males do not think chatting about life is fun. On Drew's first day of school, I thought as I buttered the toast that surely I should say something important to him on this special day. He gave me what I thought was the best entry I'd get. "Mom," he said with a mouthful of Rice Krispies, "Do you think I'll ever have a war?" Thinking he was worried that he might die on a battlefield, I launched into my best hopes for world peace and somewhat awkwardly shifted the topic to the importance of his generation becoming as well educated and civilized as possible, and this being the first day of school . . . I knew I'd already lost him, but didn't realize how soon I'd lost him until he replied, "Well, Ann said she had one on her foot and they had to cut it off."

Little girls are so aware of feelings early, I think, because they spend so much time maliciously hurting each other. Little boys, on the other hand, inflict physical pain on each other and seldom hold grudges beyond the hour. A born ameliorator, I constantly exhaust myself trying to cushion or deflect the verbal salvos they insensitively fling at one another. The abuse they heap on each other in one

hour before dinnertime would have sent me weeping to
my room for a week at their age. At bedtime when I suggest that apologies are in order so that everyone (mainly
Mom) will sleep better, neither child can recall the alter-
cation.

Their childhood is so alien to mine that from time to
time Jack feels compelled to act as an interpreter. After a
particularly destructive rampage by William, Jack says,
"Don'cha know, Mom, sometimes Willie just has to blow
up?" They have their own rituals and sacraments, I suppose, and my only mistake is in thinking they are similar
to mine. Drew said on a recent fall morning, "It's just
amazing how I'm always up for whatever season comes
along." I was all ready to join him in a hymn to September, the month of clean spiral notebooks, new beginnings,
"mists and mellow fruitfulness," when he went on to say,
"You know, I'm really ready for football just like last
spring I could hardly wait for baseball." I never measured
my seasons in sports.

What rites of passage will I see them through with special nostalgia? Buying a jockstrap isn't like buying a bra,
is it? They take so naturally to the things their father did
as a child. All three sons pile up in the bed with their dad
and listen so attentively to the Ranger baseball games on
the radio. "Nine for nineteen, Mom" Drew says as I pass
through the room. I nod, hoping he won't realize that I
don't speak the language. They worry that I never have
any fun and last winter insisted that I join them for the
Harlem Globetrotters. Well, I enjoyed the Globetrotters,
but I didn't enjoy it the way my husband did. Eyes
glued to the wizardry on the court, he'd reach across my
lap to slap one of the boys on the knee, "Now, watch this,
watch this, see how he did that. I remember this same
stunt from when I was your age and saw them at the Col-

iseum with Papa." I think I saw the Harlem Globetrotters when I was a kid, too, but all I remember is "Sweet Georgia Brown."

There is so little of my childhood to relive with them. I already know that they will never want to read *The Secret Garden, The Little Princess, Little Women,* or *Ballet Shoes.* Do boys ever keep a diary? I doubt it. Time for reflection seldom comes for a nine-year-old boy. Life is all action. Driving back from a fishing hole on a friend's farm through a field, we scared up two jackrabbits. We chased them through the field and when they disappeared, Jack said, "Sure wish we'd had a gun to shoot him." "Why would you want to do that?" I asked, thinking that the pleasure of seeing a jackrabbit had to be in seeing him hop so fast and so far. Without taking his eyes off the road, the father driving the car answered with complete understanding, "So you could see him up close."

Queen of my household? Would you ask a queen to crawl out on the roof at dawn with her middle son to watch Skylab fall on his older brother at camp thirty miles away? Do you tell the queen when she's late that she'd better put on her astroburners? Do queens spend their summers coaxing ticks from nether parts of young male bodies? My influence in this court is severely diminished now by the fact that I am female, but I am not despairing. I married a remarkable role model who assures me that all I do and say is not entirely lost on them. There are questions that will be asked that only I can answer. Jack came home last week and said that a classmate, Janet, had asked him if he liked her hair up or down. "What does that mean, Mom? Why would she think I had any opinion on her hair?" I can handle that one.

They won't grind me down, although there are days

when I stand at the top of the lovely stairway strewn with sweat socks and yell, I'm not going to live like this." Just when I'm ready to take the garbage out and keep walking, they sense it. One distracts William, the Visigoth, while the other sets the table. They pull out my chair. And the next day they pool their allowance to buy me a T-shirt that says "Heartbreaker." I'll stay. They need me. I take the long route to the soccer game so that they will have to hear Cio-Cio-San sing herself to death from Avery Fisher Hall before the kickoff.

"For it is women and the attentions they accustom us to pay them that keep up politeness and give a habit of good breeding."

—Lord Chesterfield to his son.

The Ice Cometh, Man

WILLIAM AND I were downstairs in the kitchen when it all began. For once I was glad that Willie, who is now two years old, is still a six o'clock riser. Otherwise I might not have had the coffee made. Sausage was popping in the skillet, and I even had a load of laundry in the dryer. Its heat was fogging up the windows that overlook the backyard, but I still saw the aurora borealis when half the hackberry fell across the neighbor's garage and snapped our power line. The line writhed briefly, hissing and sparking, before it came to rest on the icy ground just outside our back door. The sneakers stopped thundering in the dryer, and the little red light on the electric range went out. The rest of the coffee would be cold by the time my husband got out of bed. The steaming cup I had in my hand suddenly seemed very precious. The sausage, less than half cooked, would soon congeal in its grease.

I had just read *Cities of Vesuvius* in anticipation of the Pompeii A.D. 79 exhibit about to open at the Museum of Fine Arts in Dallas, but my personal experience with natural disasters is minimal. I grew up too far inland to get out of school for hurricanes. I've never seen a tornado, and I've always stayed clear of mobile homes in electrical

storms. Once I was in the Texas hill country when the
roads washed out, but I missed the big floods of 1978. I
have been caught in a blinding dust storm in Amarillo,
but no one there seemed to think much about it.

In spite of recent snowy winters in this part of Texas,
Dallas is still remarkably unprepared for serious weather.
None of my children has ever owned a snowsuit. Inclem-
ent weather here usually means it is raining hard enough
that I have to transport or retrieve a child from school.
Even our rain gear is sparse. I think we have one size nine
yellow rain slicker, but to my knowledge no one has ever
worn it. We somehow have always survived Dallas winters with assorted synthetic down jackets, windbreakers,
soggy sneakers with plastic bags for the snow, mateless
wool mittens, and a series of handsome black umbrellas
that all eventually get left at the courthouse by my husband. The fact is, in this comfortable, thermostatically
controlled suburb, the weather is so seldom a factor to
reckon with that we will be telling stories about our days
without power for years to come.

There is something romantic and cozy about a power
failure—at first. Feeling like a stalwart pioneer woman up
before the rest of the family stoking her wood stove, I lit
the upstairs bathroom gas wall heater, our only remaining
source of heat. An eight-branch candelabrum illuminated
our kitchen. A box of Christmas decorations had never
made it to the attic, so I retrieved red candles and the
Styrofoam frame of the Advent wreath. I also located at
least a dozen other assorted candlesticks and half-used
candles. Although it was only seven-thirty in the morning,
I was already looking forward to night, when I could
light all the candles on the mantel in the upstairs bedroom. The mirror above the mantel would double their
light, and in that glow we would read aloud.

While my imagination soared, the kitchen went dim again. William, whose eyes had danced at the lighting of the candles, had climbed up on his step stool and blown out the entire menorah. "Happy!" he squealed. "Pwesents, pwesents for Willie!" He figured it was another birthday party. I relit the candles with some difficulty. He could blow them out faster than I could light them. Trailing wax on the kitchen floor, I finally situated them safely out of his reach on top of the refrigerator. The romance of candles was beginning to fade.

Breakfast was cold cereal and sweet rolls warmed slightly on top of the water heater. The older boys, certain that the ice storm would prevent their going to church, dressed quicker than I've ever observed on a Sunday morning.

"Golleeeee! Looks like somebody dropped bombs on us last night," Drew said, surveying the huge broken limbs blocking all the driveways and sidewalks we could see from our front windows. The wind continued to whip the ice-laden trees and more limbs fell with enough force to smash a chain-link fence in our backyard. Oblivious to danger, Jack and Drew were almost giddy with delight that limbs they had despaired of ever being tall enough to climb had now bowed for them and were begging to be explored.

Family togetherness had no appeal for the boys. My candles were interesting to them only if they could strike the matches. The driveway had become an ice rink. The boys jumped back and forth from one foot to the other in the kitchen. "Please, please, let us go out." John and I eyed the power line warily. In the area of general science neither of us progressed beyond making an electromagnet with a dry-cell battery, and we operate on the premise that electricity comes from a switch plate. Would ice conduct electricity like water? We presumed it would and kept the boys inside. However, a half hour later, Jack and Drew spotted a snowsuited three-year-old and his dad in our front yard. Since we knew that the three-year-old's dad frequents hardware stores and knows how to install dimmer switches, we relented and allowed our boys outdoors with stern instructions about staying clear of the downed power line in the backyard.

All our neighbors were beginning to come out onto their porches and into their yards to assess the damage. My neighbors, for the most part, are not easily daunted. For some of these success-oriented folk, the ice storm was regarded as a gauntlet tossed. Men whose skills I thought were limited to operating Dictaphones or stethoscopes now dressed as lumberjacks, dragged ladders from their garages, and attacked their devastated trees with chain saws. A neighbor across the street was confidently beating an ice-encrusted live oak with a rubber hose. Our next-door neighbor's car was blocked in the drive by our fallen tree, and he was trying to figure out how to get it out without breaking the sprinkler heads in his lawn. We stood at our window and wondered guiltily if we should be doing something.

The house was getting a little cool by noon, so we piled into the only car that would start and went in search of a hot meal. A lot of people apparently had the same idea, and the line at Lucas B&B was far too long for a hungry two-year-old. We ended up at the takeout window of a hamburger place on Lemmon Avenue. On our way home with the lukewarm picnic, we toured the surrounding streets. Whole trees were uprooted and had fallen into Turtle Creek. Driving past our former address, we saw an old friend who had planned a New Year's Day open house. Jogging in her snow gear up to our car, she said,

"Stopping in for cold Raisin Bran tomorrow, aren't you?"
We had almost forgotten that it was New Year's Eve.

We canceled our New Year's Eve plans, even though
our hosts had heat. How could we ask a sitter to stay in a
cold, candlelit house? I later learned that a lot of New
Year's Eve plans were called off or at least altered consid-
erably. One friend, who had fifty coming for dinner,
moved the party to a neighbor's house where gas space
heaters and a gas range and a lot of candles made the celebration possible. Another group of three families wel-
comed in the new year by playing charades with their
children in front of a blazing fireplace. Hardly anyone
had a hangover the next day.

My own plans for a *Little House on the Prairie* New
Year's Eve never quite got off the ground. By 6 P.M. the
temperature in the house was 55 degrees. By my romantic
candlelight, Jack tripped and fell down the stairs, landing
on his head. My children are not noted for stoic behavior
when they get hurt, so it is difficult to determine the extent of injury by asking them. By flashlight I reread Dr.
Spock's remarks on brain concussion. How could I possibly determine if the child's eyes were dilated? All of our
eyes were dilated in the darkening house. I also suspected
that Jack had read up on concussions. He took to his bed
complaining dramatically that his head felt like it had an-
tennas and he was receiving from alien planets.

For New Year's Eve dinner, we huddled around the
single heater in the upstairs bathroom and ate franchise
pepperoni and mushroom pizza. Drew angled the flashlight so he could carefully pick the mushrooms off his
portion. I found the mushrooms days later, clinging like
dried snails to the sides of the bathroom wastebasket.

Everyone was irritable after dinner. The candles by
that time had dripped all over everything. John diag-

nosed his cold as bronchitis and said that the whole scene was beginning to remind him of his basic training at Fort Leonard Wood. In sleeping bags, several pairs of pajamas, and socks, the entire family was bedded down by nine o'clock.

William was the first one up on New Year's Day. Worried that even three pairs of pajamas wouldn't keep him warm enough, I had moved him to a spare twin bed with me shortly before midnight. He slept fine; I didn't. At dawn, he sat up, pulled the cover off, and announced, "All gone! Toast, juice!" Then he yanked the pull chain of the reading light on the headboard and yelled, "Light! Work! Mom, get tool man. Won't work!"

After drinking tepid tap-water tea by the bathroom heater and trying to make hot chocolate in a silver coffee pot with a candle warmer, we concluded that we had made the pioneer effort, but our resources were too limited. We reviewed our options at Kip's Big Boy Restaurant, where I deliberately took a table beside two men who had arrived in a panel truck and who wore elaborate tools on their belts. I offered them our Sunday paper and tried lamely to discuss the upcoming Cotton Bowl game with them. Finally one of them grinned at me and said, "Lady, is it your phone?" "No, my power line." "Sorry," he said, "we're just phones."

Our friend who had offered Raisin Bran called when we returned to the cold house to say that her power had been restored and we should plan to bring the whole family for a hot lunch. With our thermostat registering 45 degrees, we began to load our car with sleeping bags, pillows, crib mattresses, Teddy bears, extra blankets, and snack food. We were strange urban nomads in search of a house with something more than a bathroom heater.

Our first stop was the New Year's Day open house. The

hardships of the storm relieved everyone of the pressure of having to look chic. No one even noticed my flared jeans with the thermal underwear making a full break over my tennis shoes. The open house had been transformed into a neighborhood Salvation Army. Besides getting my whole family fed there, I did laundry and bathed a baby. Cold, bewildered toddlers we couldn't even identify were being deposited at the front door by parents who murmured something about coming back for them when things warmed up a bit. Some people watched ball games on television, but I sensed that those of us without any power in our homes felt TV watching to be conspicuous consumption.

Our hosts begged us to stay the night, but since they already had five children of their own, we opted to impose on a young bachelor friend that first night away from home. Etiquette was totally ignored. Against my better judgment, John impulsively called and said, "Huff, you have heat? Good, we're cold, and we're spending the night with you tonight." Huff's house was spacious and warm enough, but decidedly spartan to those of us accustomed to the clutter of a large family. His immaculate kitchen was equipped with one skillet, two cereal bowls, three forks, a broken can opener, and no coffee maker. His television set, a small, flickering black-and-white, was inadequate to hold the attention of three restless little boys, so they bounced off the walls. We hadn't realized what a crowd we made, particularly in a dwelling accustomed to only one. I apologized a lot. The next morning, when his bathroom pipes had frozen and my sons discovered it *after* they had both used the toilet, we quietly lowered the lid, packed our chaos, and moved on.

Next, we shamelessly invited ourselves to move in with dear old friends whom we had not seen as often as we intended in the past year. No matter how much our families might have diverged in that time, we concluded that in homes with children certain noise levels and patterns of living are constant. Somehow we knew that our three boys would mesh comfortably with their two boys, nervous dog, and two goldfish. At least there would be a coffeepot and more than a quart of milk in the refrigerator.

Although there was still a great deal of ice, our lawyer husbands resumed work and school opened for a few hours that Tuesday. Their house was quieter than usual with four boys gone. Even Baby William occupied himself feeding crackers to the nervous dog while my friend and I drank tea and renewed a nine-year friendship that might otherwise have faded in the busyness of our respective routines. Willie napped and the children gradually filtered in from school. Drew contented himself by watching Lance and Goldie, the goldfish, and spent considerable time at the piano. The other boys played football in the double stairwell, and despite our warnings and threats, at least one child walked on the irresistible frozen blue-green swimming pool in the backyard. Jack, my type A child, who lays out his clothes for school with the belt already in the loops of his jeans, searched the house frantically for an alarm clock. No one complained that there was nothing to do. That evening, with nine of us around the dining room table, we felt like one big compatible family. The ice storm no longer seemed so malevolent.

During our three days away from home, we had to make periodic trips back to the house to get extra clothing, to check for frozen pipes, and to feed the cat, who remained like a frozen sentinel in the living room. I felt like Swiss Family Robinson returning to the wrecked ship to salvage useful items. Without electricity our modern conveniences had become steely, cold hunks of junk. The electric range, the toaster, the Christmas Cuisinart, the juicer, the trendy coffee grinder, even my electric typewriter, all reproached us on each visit. In the bitter cold, I even loathed my new house. Why did I ever think those large windows were lovely? Who wanted cross ventilation? My plants were frozen, the cat had spilled his food all over the kitchen floor, and I didn't investigate to see which potted plant he had used as a litter box. Dirty dishes remained unwashed in the sink. Two days' clutter of clothing, shoes, and pajamas lay on the floors. No one had picked up in the dark, and, since the temperature in the house continued to drop, no one would unglove a hand to do it on our foraging trips.

Although the dead power line remained unattached in our backyard, we still couldn't adjust to the fact that we had no electricity. I kept trying to turn on closet lights. A friend admitted to me that on one of the long, cold days in her house, she decided to use the thawing strawberries in her freezer to make smoothies for her kids. She tossed the makings in her blender before remembering that it wouldn't work. Her kids thought it was hilarious. She shrugged her shoulders, then tossed the whole mess down her electric disposal. The pipes in one of our bathrooms froze and a helpful neighbor suggested that I use my hair dryer to thaw them.

According to Dallas Power & Light, 75,000 homes in Dallas were without electrical power. I heard of one man who injured his foot kicking the electronic garage door which held both of his cars prisoner. Many were undoubtedly far worse off than he was or we were. The ingenious ways people kept warm put us to shame. One friend employed her grandmother's method, which she recalled from her childhood in Italy during World War II. "We took coals and ashes from the fireplace and put them in big cans with holes punched in them to warm the cold bedrooms," she told me. "But where did you find the big cans?" I asked, thinking of our household of plastic containers. "Oh, we used the cans the swimming pool chemicals come in." When the ingenuity ran out, and Dallas Power & Light continued to give a busy signal, some women went out independently in search of help. One glamorous friend admitted that when she spotted two green DP&L trucks on Boedeker Drive, she turned in to a side street, reapplied her makeup, put on her daughter's rabbit-fur coat, and then pulled up beside the seemingly unoccupied line repairmen. "Hi there!" she said, smiling. "You fellows wanna come to my house and see about my lines?" Hers got repaired that afternoon while the rest of us listened to DP&L's recorded message.

On the fourth day my next-door neighbor called to report that lights were on at my house. For us, the crisis was over. Others would remain without power twice as long. Being without heat was miserable, and I can't glamorize it, but at the same time the ice storm forced us to start the new year with fewer illusions about ourselves. For all of our jogging, vitamins, and exercise classes, we are not very strong when stripped of our push buttons and switch plates. And our children are even worse. They don't even know how to respect the flames in a gas heater. I had never properly appreciated flame-retardant fabric until I smelled Drew's coat melting while he stood warming his backside. In the twenty-four hours we huddled by that gas heater, we scorched a small laminated stool where mittens were drying and lost one white plastic wastebasket (Drew was cracking pecans in it by the heater and, when I picked up the basket to empty it, it looked like a taffy pull). We confess that we know little about preventive measures when it comes to maintaining a house through a severe winter. I'm determined to find the water cutoff before next year. For a few weeks after the storm, we were almost superstitious about energy consumption. Each closet light seemed a miracle, and hardly anyone had to be reminded to turn lights off.

There was a run on the Army-Navy store after the storm subsided. I even bought insulated rubber boots for the older boys and a new round of gloves for the whole family. Coleman lanterns, butane stoves, and all sorts of battery-powered equipment sold out in one day. A woman in the grocery store told me that her husband had already installed a generator so that they would never be caught without power again. Ironically, although some of us had spent memorable times with our neighbors and friends during those four days, here we were trying to be self-sufficient again, trying to squeeze life back into a well-planned checklist with no surprises.

Part Three

Firstborn

Plant a carrot, get a carrot,
Not a brussels sprout.
That's why I love vegetables,
You know what you're about.
—*The Fantasticks*

JACK SOMETIMES runs with his Dad at the university track near our house on Sunday afternoons. I love to watch them. While John's running is rhythmically paced, Jack's is more like a dance. He runs with such exuberance, turning and running backward a few yards as if to see where he's been; then he leaps into the air like a spirited mustang colt and sprints forward again. The wind in his face parts his shiny brown hair in the middle, and when he joins me in the car with his face so flushed, he looks like a small Robert Redford groomed for *The Great Gatsby*. I know that his seemingly perfect proportion, flawless skin, and graceful coordination for a preadolescent are fleeting, so I try to look hard at him from time to time so I won't forget.

It hardly seems possible that I've known him for nine years. Of the three boys, the firstborn is the most aloof. He does not take to easy intimacy the way his brothers have. He has inherited his father's restraint, and although it confounds me, I respect it.

Girls have noticed Jack, but he has noticed only their alien behavior. He stripped their carefully selected Valentines of lollipops without ever reading the timid P.S.s penciled on the back. He insists that Drew take any incoming phone calls from females. "Jack, this is Karen on the phone. She wants to know if you love Courtney," Drew relays to Jack. Jack shakes his head emphatically. Drew, with total deadpan expression says, "My brother said to tell you, 'No way, José.'"

Jack tells me with some bewilderment that fourth-grade girls at his school carry purses with lip gloss and breath spray and that they giggle in the girls' rest room when they're supposed to be changing shoes for gym class. Astutely, he has noted, "There are just a few girls at Armstrong that you can trust." Despite the gap between his ripply front teeth, I think I might have written his name on my book cover if he'd been in my fourth-grade class.

He once wrote my name on a pasteboard box in his room. Scrawled in angry red crayon were the words "I hayt Mom." Because he and I are locked into this mother-firstborn-son relationship, we seem destined to be either butting heads or renewing truce agreements with tearful exhausted embraces.

I've always approached clinical studies of personality development with considerable skepticism. Although I cannot resist sizing up myself or my family members in Sunday-supplement pop psychology quizzes, I still prefer to believe our respective passages (beyond the "terrible twos," which I have documented three times), life crises, and general quirky behavior are unique. The suggestion that a child's personality is determined by his position in the family flies in the face of my free spirit.

Nevertheless, shortly after my third son was born, I did read *The Birth Order Factor* by Lucille Forer. Firstborn children, she reports, usually exhibit (1) high need for achievement, (2) high responsibility, (3) strong self-discipline, (4) need for approval from others, (5) susceptibility to social pressure, (6) conformity to authority, and (7) task orientation. Her report also suggests that firstborns are usually well suited to becoming military leaders or astronauts.

Military leaders or astronauts? No wonder we butt heads. When he was born, my ambitions for him were probably just short of Renaissance Man. In the rocking chair I made up melodies for "Jack Be Nimble," "Little Jack Horner," and "This Is the House That Jack Built"; he responded with percussive air raid sounds and says now he might be willing to sing in the church choir if it pays minimum wage. I sent him to the museum art school to spatter paint like Jackson Pollock, and he saved his allowance to buy protractors and T squares to draw straighter lines. How far is it from "the stuff that dreams are made of" to the *Right Stuff?*

I suppose I should have caught on, the day we were foolishly discussing "good mothers we have known." Jack cut the idle speculation by saying, "Well, you know the perfect mother is probably an orphanage. You know, everything is on schedule, meals at a certain time, laundry done, study time, lights out." I was momentarily aghast, but I suppose Dr. Forer wouldn't be. Jack's statement probably capsules the problem rigid firstborn sons have with mellow second-born moms.

Jack is fastidious to a fault. His room is as spare and

clean as a monk's cell. He even insisted on moving the matching twin bed out of his room because it was "unnecessary." Spend-the-night company, he explained, could use the neatly rolled sleeping bag and air mattress in his closet. By dumping piles of books (my favorites), toys (the Creative Playthings recorder, and the "useless Legos with lost instructions"), he pared the clutter on his bookshelves down to encyclopedias (woe to the brother who borrows one and stuffs it back in the shelf at random), a dictionary, three books about space, two about sports, C. S. Lewis's *The Chronicles of Narnia*, which he may yet discover are a bit fanciful for his taste, a record player, a small microscope, and his Instamatic camera. His desk has perfectly aligned rulers, protractors, paper, and sharpened pencils.

His discipline is phenomenal. No, it's like his slightly compulsive father's (an only child). And I suppose, wallowing in my characteristic clutter and procrastination, I occasionally covet it. He comes home from school, fixes a snack, shoots baskets, or watches television for exactly fifteen minutes, then goes to his room, closes the door, and does his homework—very neatly. Before I signed his perfect report card last term, he said, "Mom, could you try a little harder with your cursive this time?"

We are so different. He likes computers; I don't even like self-winding watches. He likes modern houses with square lines and shiny hi-tech furniture. The house we live in is sixty years old, and our inherited furniture is Victorian. I like fresh-squeezed orange juice; he prefers a chewable vitamin C tablet.

Like a good astronaut, he likes to check off lists and obey rules. I like to make rules and lists, but I frequently lose them. When we moved to the new house, I announced that life was going to be different. With a two-

story house and no curtains downstairs, we'd just have to
come to the breakfast table dressed. No more slopping
around in pajamas at eight o'clock. And perhaps on Tuesdays everybody should strip their beds and bring the
dirty sheets downstairs. Breakfast would be served
promptly at seven-thirty. I even drew up menus—French
toast on Monday, eggs on Tuesday, oatmeal, etc. I par-
celed out garbage duty, table-setting, and dishwasher-
unloading detail. I even typed the new regimen on clean
white bond and taped it on the refrigerator door. Jack
was ecstatic. You'd have thought I'd just been cast as a
Stepford wife.

I lasted about a week. Tuesday of the second week,
Jack stood alone in the breakfast room downstairs with
his hair combed, teeth brushed, backpack strapped on,
and bedclothes piled at his feet. "Where's the scrambled
eggs?" he yelled up the stairs. "It's seven thirty-two."

The real capper, however, came one night when I was
reading *Tom Sawyer* aloud to Jack and Drew. We had
reached a point where Tom and Huck were planning to
swing dead cats in a graveyard at midnight. "Wait a minute," Jack interrupted, "they can't do that. Boys their age
would have to be in bed at nine o'clock." Does a mother
have the right to give her eldest son the raspberry?

In *The Birth Order Factor*, Dr. Forer says that firstborn
children develop their law-abiding natures because, alone
with their parents at first, they receive the full brunt of
parental scrutiny and authority. Even if the parents are
not terribly demanding, the firstborn child has only adults
by which to measure his own performance. Later-born
children, especially if they are in the company of siblings
with similarly lousy coordination, seldom berate themselves about spilled milk.

My own self-pressuring firstborn tears up his homework

if he makes an error, hits himself on the head when he can't immediately grasp a math concept and refuses any assistance or comfort if he trips over a chair. "I'm holding it in," he yells, fighting tears; "it's dumb to cry." Creative assignments are anathema to such a perfectionist. He wants answers that can be checked in the back of the book with rewards handed out fairly. "How do you know if your dumb poem is right?" he asks. If I harbor any illusions about his wanting to follow my journalistic bent, I have only to recall the day the mail brought a newsy letter from his eight-year-old buddy who had recently moved to the West Coast. I explained that such a letter certainly required a response and probably expounded at length about the pleasure of maintaining such correspondence with an old friend. Under duress, Jack went to his room and returned with this epistle:

> Deer Peter,
>
> Don't rite me eny moore.
>
> Your fried,
>
> Jack

At PTA open house, John and I, who have excessive print addiction, were shocked to learn that our son is the only one in the whole fourth grade who refused to read ten books for membership in the Texas Reader's Club. "It was optional, Mom," he shrugs.

I had always thought that pressured children only sprung from fathers who stand on the sidelines of fourth-grade football fields and yell, "I'm gonna kick your butt from here to Fort Worth if that man comes over your hole again." We never yelled anything at Jack's soccer games. In fact, I once said to him on the way to a game, "Jack, I hope you know that your daddy and I want you to have fun playing soccer and we really don't care whether you win or lose." He fixed me with a steely glance and said, "Mom, my coach has taught me good skills, and I play to win whether you care or not."

A friend once told me that she tries very hard to have no expectations for her children. "I don't want them ever to think that they've disappointed me." I think she is expecting the impossible from herself. Our very presence is a pressure most people of my generation never felt from their own parents. As children of Depression parents whose educations were often cut short by financial need, we had only to obtain a college degree or perhaps a secure job to fulfill their wildest ambitions for us. It was easy for us to grow up with the notion that children always outstrip their parents in achievement.

Somehow we expect our children to do more than we did, but it's unclear even to us just what that "more" could be. We do not have the same illusions about professions that our parents' generation had. We know enough frustrated doctors and lawyers to know that a graduate degree is no guarantee of a good life. Nevertheless, we will be just as anxious that they avoid the pitfalls that we perceive in our own experiences.

When I was in college I read a collection of F. Scott Fitzgerald's letters to his daughter Scottie, many of which were written in the waning years of his life. Fearful that he had not fulfilled his own potential, Fitzgerald composed these stern yet loving letters as if he were writing to himself as a young man at Princeton. The letters are filled with the wisdom of hindsight ("Don't take the courses that you know you can make an 'A' in. You'll learn those things on your own. Your mother never knew how to use her energy—she's passed that failing on to you. I have felt all my life the absence of hobbies. . . . And after reading Thoreau I felt how much I have lost by leaving nature out of my life."). I read his letters as if my own father had written them and took much of his advice to heart. His own daughter, on the other hand, admitted in the preface that she had checked the letters for money, then tossed them unread into a bottom drawer. I suppose the real wisdom to be gained from those letters is precisely that. My children will probably seek their wisdom elsewhere.

I still try to get my two cents' worth in where I can with Jack. Since he already seems destined to be a type A, I'm better off listening, recounting my own foibles, and hugging him when I can get away with it. Because he once hurled his digital watch against a wall in a fit of temper, he loves to hear that in a similar pique I once cut a hole in my favorite dress. As for the hugging, my younger sons are regular lapdogs. But with Jack, the last good mutual squeeze was in the doctor's office nearly a year ago. In the privacy of that examination room waiting for a booster shot, this gangly, long-legged nine-year-old trembled in my lap like a two-year-old. Once the shot was over, however, he cleared his eyes, squared his shoulders, and looked at me as if to say, "I won't need you for this again."

The best of the conversations with him invariably come at bedtime when the light is out. Only then do I stand a chance of hearing the small and not so small humiliations of his day. The conversations are mostly stream of consciousness, but they make me remember that a large part of childhood was self-conscious embarrassment—particularly for little achievers who try so hard to keep everything under control. "Mom, do you think William will be the kind of boy who likes to clean up and keep things neat?"

"I don't know, Jack." (I seem to say that a lot.)

"Well, I know he's gonna be a sports boy because that runs in the family." (What sort of sports hero story has his 158-pound father been fabricating?)

"School okay today?" I ask casually.

"No, it was horrible. Miss Turner made me dance with her in music"—a folk dance, I presume—"and the whole class laughed and when we got back to class to take our spelling test, I didn't hear one of the words and Joe yelled out, '*Dance*, Jack, like you and Miss Turner like to do.' After school I had to kick him till he cried. I hate Miss Turner, I hate music . . . and I will never go to church when I'm grown because they make you sing in the choir and"—by this time there were tears—"I will never play in the band even though Dad will force me and I've been hating you for three weeks. . . ."

Exhausted at the end of the day, too, I bear these diatribes with whatever equanimity I have left. With his younger brothers I can cajole and heal with the casual affections of eyes and hands, but their burdens are not so heavy. They don't report dreams about Anwar Sadat or list inflation as one of their greatest concerns. Jack does. The younger boys increase his burden by standing in awe of him. They know that he walks first where they may walk someday. The power he has over them is probably small recompense for the pains of having to go first. They will turn cartwheels in the territory he explored so cautiously. On the way to the swimming pool, it has never occurred to them to worry "What if I've forgotten 'jumping in'?"

I demand too much of him because he is so responsible. And as a younger sibling once myself, I overreact to his taunting of younger brothers. When he senses injustice, he meets my reprimand with a stare so belligerent, so shriveling that, though I seldom back down, I spend hours privately reviewing his case. I am still much too soft for adolescence.

So I'm trying to look hard at him right now. I like to see him run unleashed with the wind in his hair. I don't worry then about who he'll turn out to be. I just like who he is.

Middle Child

But many that are first shall
be last; and the last shall be
first.
—*Matthew 19:30*

I'm never first and I'm never
last.
Drew Mackintosh,
the middle child

DREW IS seven years old now. I have a few pictures to
prove that he was once a baby, but almost no memories.
He never received the sort of total attention and applause
that firstborns and perhaps babies-of-the-family claim as a
matter of course. I had the flu the day of his first-grade
Christmas pageant this year, and although I rallied
enough to make his Indian costume out of a horrible
piece of vinyl material (I didn't have the heart to tell him
that without the feathers he looked more like a Lazy-Boy
recliner), his nine-year-old brother was the only family
member in the audience. While Nikons whir for
firstborns, even the Tooth Fairy has been known to forget
to fly for this in-between son.

From the very beginning it was as if Drew acceded to

his older brother's wish, "No upstaging, please." Drew
was the pleasant sort of baby who quickly slept through
the night and ate on schedule with a minimum of fuss. I
recently watched a home movie labeled "Drew's Chris-
tening Party." The film contains extensive footage of two-
year-old Jack playing peek-a-boo from behind a chair,
some nice shots of guests, grandparents, and priest, but
only one brief sweep of the honoree asleep in his crib.

Any two-year-old is tough competition for a scrawny,
toothless newborn. In Drew's early years, the limelight
remained firmly fixed on the dancy-eyed Jack lisping the
story of the Little Red Caboose to an adoring audience
awed by what in our inexperience we took to be precocity. Drew even obliged by being born with a fright wig
of black hair so unruly that when I carried him at five
weeks past the storefront windows in the shopping center, my favorite barber bolted out of his shop to give
Drew his first haircut free right there on the sidewalk.
Somehow when Ray Haden parted this peculiar thick baby
hair and slicked it down with a little barbershop pomade,
Drew looked like a tiny, very serious middle-aged man.
Small wonder that at age six he told the innocents in his
car pool that he was actually a forty-five-year-old midget
who supports himself on gin rummy winnings.

At seven he is still a child for the discerning. His
charms are subtle. Though the fright wig was long ago
exchanged for thick Hyannis Port hair, Sunday photog-
raphers do not instinctively snap his picture in the park.
He is now sandwiched between two flashy beauties. Jack
at nine, despite his ridged and gapped permanent teeth,
still has the large Bambi eyes, a gazelle-like grace and
symmetrical proportions so easy to admire. William at
three is a fairer copper-haired, blue-eyed version of Jack
with an irresistible, impish quality that enables him to

win the heart of even the grocery store stock boy who is still mopping Wesson Oil spilled on our last visit.

Drew's face has never had the look of spontaneous joy and innocence generally associated with childhood. He smirks a lot for a kid his age, does fair imitations of Groucho Marx, and is likely to ask the music teacher at school if she knows a catchy little tune called "Jada." Of his kindergarten class he said, "It's okay, Mom, but I just have to stare at the floor when that teacher says 'Cock-a-doodle-doo, I know what to do.'" The day he portrayed Jesus entering Jerusalem triumphant on a donkey in the school pageant, his bathrobe gaped to reveal his Steve Martin T-shirt imprinted with "Just a Wild and Crazy Guy." I know that he frustrated his nursery-school teachers who need smiling reinforcement as much as their charges. He was the only child in his kindergarten room who could do twenty minutes of Body Rhythms—hopping, skating, skipping, and clapping to lively music with a totally deadpan expression. When I told him point-blank that I thought he should fake a smile or two for his teacher's sake, he replied, "But, Mom, I'm trying to make the Guinness Book of World Records for frowning since birth."

Drew is also left-handed, an affliction which we right-handed parents have hypocritically played up as a special God-given talent. We have assured him that his career as a first baseman is secure and that no one expects a lefty on the basketball courts. I have even attributed his un-canny ability to find lost items to his left-handedness. However, he is already discovering, with some assistance from Jack, that Southpaws, excepting Leonardo, of course, are most likely to be "bad drawers in art class" and "very dumb meatcutters."

Asked about his best friends, Drew would probably list

his big brother first (he would never appear on big brother's list); then his barber; the Slurpee clerk at the 7-11; an American Airline pilot who used to be our neighbor; Ozzie, the crossing guard, and an odd assortment of animals. At a Christmas open house this year, he tugged at my arm and whispered, "Can I go upstairs? There's somebody up there I need to see." I later learned it was a gerbil whose acquaintance he had made while I had a lengthy conversation with the hostess several months earlier. Drew is the son most likely to come banging in the back door announcing that he has made two new friends on the way home from school. When I ask their names, he says, "Well, one is tan and one is spotted." He is quiet and patient enough to teach our surly tomcat to walk on its hind legs for a cracker. When I am late to retrieve him from his piano lesson, he says, "That's okay, Mom, it just gave me a chance to get in a good visit with Mrs. Kaesler's dogs." He has elaborate theories on how to converse with animals. I have watched nervously from the front porch as he walks home from the corner with two unknown golden retrievers licking his cheeks and almost knocking him to the ground. "They're sorta rough, Mom," he says, "but did you see how much they love me?"

Drew's gentle manner not only endears him to the St. Francis of Assisi crowd; his popularity with the mothers of his friends is legend. He's well liked by his classmates, but I suspect he gets invited home with classmates on rainy days because their moms know that he is least likely to engineer games like Tarzan of the Drapes or Bunk Bed Trampoline. He will play Monopoly, gin rummy, or crazy eight longer than anyone wants to.

Of course, I sometimes worry that this flexible nature and remarkable patience could also be interpreted as languor or just laziness. Teaching the cat to dance on his hind legs is easier than opening a can of cat food. Although his quick wit and his hard-earned smiles suggest that he marches to a different drummer, I sometimes suspect that he is ambling down the path of least resistance. After an inspiring unit on the instruments of the orchestra, his nursery-school teacher asked each student what instrument he would wish to play when he was old enough. Drew replied, "A stereo."

Ask him what famous person he'd like to be, however, and Drew will invariably say "Jack, my big brother." No ambition could be more farfetched. They are poles apart in their respective approaches to life. Jack, the firstborn tortoise, disciplines himself and achieves according to the puritan work ethic, while Drew arrives at his finish lines quite by chance. Jack memorized math facts by doggedly reviewing flash cards. Drew learned his being the banker in Monopoly or playing poker with his grandparents. Jack dutifully does his chores to earn an allowance while Drew seems to keep his pockets jingling with change won in football-game wagers or dimes left in phone booths. When other first-graders are busily computing on their fingers, Drew astounds the teacher by announcing that "Thirteen plus thirteen equals twenty-six." "How did you guess?" the teacher asks. "My shoes told me," he says. "That's why I like to wear my soccer shoes—thirteen cleats on each shoe."

And, of course, he's a dreamer. He infuriates nightmare-plagued Jack at bedtime by ordering his dreams aloud. "Tonight," he says, "we'll have some monkeys, some balloons, a bald-headed dwarf, one robot, and no spiders." After reading Beverly Cleary's *Mouse and the Motorcycle,* he carefully laid out a small matchbox motorcycle and a half-ping-pong-ball helmet in various corners of his room hoping for similar adventures with rodents at our house. He swears that his dream techniques are effective and perhaps they are. I can't recall his ever having a nightmare, and sometimes the unfinished dreams are so fabulous that I find him in bed after breakfast trying to finish them.

For all of his apparent insouciance, life is not all beautiful dreams and wisecracks for Drew. The business of being neither first nor last is never easy, and no seven-year-old handles it with equanimity all the time. As I boarded a plane for New York last summer, my husband yelled, "And for Pete's sake, don't bring Drew anything that Jack wants or that Willie could break." Drew knows tears and frustrations that I can only half understand, being a second child, but never a middle. His precocious drollness backfires with childish malapropisms. "Just *admire* my baby brother, he's just trying to get some attention." And his sophistication vanishes in a torrent of abuse from his adored big brother. "I am dumb. Jack says I'm dumb. I know I am. Miss Jones lies and puts 'Wow' on my papers, but Jack knows I'm really dumb."

I'm not sure when or if little brothers outgrow the stigma of their older brothers' opinion. And when I try to salve his wounded ego, I am dismissed with, "Yeah and you're the mother who used to like those cats I drew with seven legs." Perhaps I've just always had a taste for eccentrics, but I can't help feeling that regardless of how much he loses by virtue of his position in the family, he still wins. Lefties have always had to adapt, but middle lefties develop special survival skills that can only benefit them in adult life.

Drew, if someday you are negotiating Middle East settlements with style and humor, I will tell the reporters that you were ever the comic relief between two headstrong sons; that you fished empty ponds with your Dad without complaining; that you had a penchant for stepping in dog pies; that you agreed to take piano lessons only because I bribed you with Slurpees and then you proceeded to play like Hoagy Carmichael while looking over your shoulder to see cartoons on television; that you held firm with your little brother and made a decent human being out of him even when your mom yelled, "Let the baby have it." Maybe I will even tell them how much I needed you, and how I panicked one day when I thought you were gone. I returned paint to the hardware store and left you in the car once when you were six. I returned to an empty car and figured you had gone window shopping. A half dozen little old ladies emerging from a dress shop heard me calling your name and joined me in my search, only they were yelling, "Bruce, Bruce, where are you?" After fifteen minutes, just as I was on the verge of calling the police, you emerged with characteristic nonchalance from M. E. Moses Variety Store. The little ladies gathered around you reprovingly and said, "Now, Bruce, there's your mother. What do you have to say for yourself? She was worried half to death. Why didn't you answer when we called you in that store?" You rolled your eyes heavenward and sighed, "Because my name is Drew and I was in the toilet."

Three's Company

"AIN'T IT funny how some babies jus' show up bein' comp'ny," my friend's housekeeper said, looking at tiny three-week-old William. He grinned his absurd little grin, and I couldn't help thinking, "Yeah, and at two o'clock this morning, I didn't even know I was lonely."

Other than the initial loss of sleep, William's impact on us was gradual. Perhaps if he'd been the girl that everyone had wished on us this third time around, we would have made a bigger fuss about him right from the first. He required no new layette and slept so regularly in those early months that I often forgot he was there. More than once I pulled away from the curb with the two older boys on a grocery-store run only to remember that my third son was still asleep in his crib in the back room. We once took William out to dinner with us, and he slept so peacefully in his infant carrier under the table that after we'd paid the check and zipped the older boys in their coats at the door, the waitress clearing our table yelled, "Hey, don't you want your baby?"

William, the baby born in our thirties, was what one might call a great leap of faith. Two children just seemed a little too statistically average American family. All around us people were dramatically discarding spouses, launching new careers, or becoming "urban pioneers" in slum neighborhoods. I seem to recall that there was much talk in 1976 of needing to take risks in order to grow. Content in our marriage, careers, and neighborhood, having a third child seemed an adequately perilous venture. I don't think we seriously believed that we might produce a girl, but perhaps the possibility was also a factor in our foolhardiness.

Jack and Drew were reasonably civilized four- and six-year-olds when William was born. At thirty-two, I was no longer surrounded by conscientious young mothers, and somehow after that four-year interim between second and third babies, I never quite got into the swing of tiny infants. William and I frequently left home without extra diapers or bottles. Wash-and-wear fabrics were no longer deemed fashionable in '76, and without spit-up pads, my natural fibers were gradually cemented on the right shoulders with Gerber's teething biscuit drool. William learned to eat peanut butter sandwiches very early because I instinctively rolled past the baby food displays at the grocery store.

I was not irresponsible. I was just relaxed. My pediatrician, who had only two children of his own, had begun to seek my advice. After seeing two sons survive my seldom sterilized mothering, I didn't panic when six-month-old William and I were stranded three hours at an airport without bottles or baby food. We just went into the airport restaurant and shared vegetable soup.

Far from being a neglected baby, Willie was more like a firstborn with four people instead of two applauding his every move. Drew and Jack were old enough to be more fascinated than threatened by this blue-eyed newcomer who responded to their attention by inhaling and crowing simultaneously as if he were trying to swallow them both. We spent many a hilarious afternoon making up silly stories about helpless William, the little man with no teeth. Drew delighted in asking him where he'd left his dentures. Sometimes I'd hold him under his arms over a table, and when he stretched his legs in that peculiar marching reflex, Jack and Drew would sing "It's a treat to beat your feet on the Mississippi mud" or aim water guns at his feet and yell, "Reach for the skies, podnah, we're gonna make you dance," until they fell out totally convulsed with laughter. I even let them paint heavy Groucho eyebrows on him with my eyebrow pencil one rainy afternoon. Babies make terrific straight men.

But our days were not all crowing and singing. I recorded in my notebook on December 30 (William would have been a month old) a day so horrible that I wonder how I kept my head out of the oven.

The water heater was broken—leaking on the floor—and the plumber brought the new one at eight-thirty before I was dressed. In all of the confusion I was still in my robe at ten when the installation was finished. Decided to bathe Willie before getting dressed. As soon as I put him in the tub, the phone rang. I yelled at Jack and Drew to answer it. Drew tried to reach the phone in the baby's room, but because he used the open drawers of the chest as a stepladder, he pulled the whole chest over on himself, dumping telephone and two pot plants into a drawer of clean diapers. Whoever called never called back.

When William was dressed, Drew comforted, and the diapers in the washing machine again, it was nearly noon. Still in my robe, I packed sack lunches for the two older boys and suggested that they have a picnic on the school grounds a block away. Once they were out of the house I dressed, fed William and took him for a little fresh air in

the stroller. Drew spotted me as I turned the corner by
the school. "Mom," he yelled in a desperate tone, "I
spilled my thermos." "Cope," I yelled back, and quickly
headed back to the house.

Moments later Drew, sobbing, banged in the back
door. "Are you still crying about that thermos?" I asked.
"No," he hiccuped. "The school building wasn't open and
I wet my pants."

Without any guilt at all, I let Jack and Drew watch
Godzilla versus King Kong while I washed my hair and
lay down for a nap.

I woke up abruptly. William was crying, and Drew
was screaming from the bathroom that he had diarrhea
and couldn't get to the bathroom fast enough. Jack was
dancing around the bathroom pointing at his stricken
brother and taunting "Mama mia, Papa pee-a, Drew has
got the diarrhea." I banished Jack to his room, cleaned
up Drew as best I could, dropped the soiled underwear
in the toilet to soak, then rescued my hungry infant. In
the meantime, Drew makes it to the toilet unassisted, but
before I could warn him, he, of course, flushed the underwear. Because this wasn't the first inappropriate item to
be flushed at our house, the toilet overflowed.

5:30 P.M.: John wants to know what's for supper.
Maybe if the plumber comes at nine o'clock tomorrow . . .

We were outnumbered. Three children is many more
than two, and our (I'm no martyr—John's too) resources,
both physical and emotional, were often strained to the
breaking point.

Perhaps that's why William's baptism was the most fes-
tive of any we'd ever had. Never before had we been
quite so willing to humbly admit our inadequacy and to
wholeheartedly enlist the "Aid of all who need." The
guests, the food, the flowers, and the church ceremony

were a unique affirmation of our inability to cope alone. For this occasion, we purposefully returned on a misty spring morning to the Episcopal church in Austin where John and I had met and later were married. The guests were drawn from our past—parents, cousins, boarding-school teachers, classmates, and college friends; from our present—lawyers, neighbors, writers, and magazine editors; and perhaps from the future—the children of all assembled. At the godparents' house, a lacquered Tibetan umbrella topped their antique carousel and silk flags flew from the heads of the weathered wooden horses. The godfather, another William, supplied fine champagne, and guests brought azaleas, iris, and forsythia from their own yards for the outside buffet tables laden with beautiful food I did not try to prepare myself—spinach-and-mushroom quiche, exquisite breads baked in butterfly shapes, and ceviche surrounded by avocados, marinated carrots, and beets. A small chocolate rabbit cake for the children said "Welcome William" in white icing. At the baptism itself our contemporaries, who perhaps in their agnostic twenties donned Groucho noses at wedding ceremonies, now participated solemnly as we collectively renounced, "by God's help, the devil and all his works, the vain pomp and glory with all covetous desires of the same and sinful desires of the flesh."

William, now three years old, has been the bane and blessing of our existence. As Robert Capon once wrote of his youngest daughter, "Destruction is in her hands, and desolation in the paths of her feet; She spoileth all their pleasant things." Perhaps William's older brothers were just as incorrigible and we have forgotten because our "pleasant things" then were not so precious. Child of our thirties, he never knew the '65 Chevrolet, the upstairs duplex, or the mother with magazine deadlines and no

household help. Because a mother of three has less tolerance for grocery store tantrums, he usually gets the bubble gum I so scrupulously denied the other two at his age.
In his terrorizing twos, he instituted a sort of "Catch-22"
principle at our house wherein to get the dishwasher
unloaded, I allowed him to fling disposable diapers all
over the kitchen; to get the diapers collected I banished
him to the upstairs study, where he unboxed and decorated two dozen envelopes; while I salvaged the station-
ery, he dropped playing cards quietly down the stairwell;
and when the cards were reboxed I found him waxing the
nightstand with cuticle cream. I have whacked his behind
harder and more frequently than his brothers' with less
penitent results. He resolutely goes about his toddler
business—the distributing of small piles of unrelated objects—a graham cracker piece, my perfume bottle top, two
hair clips, a puzzle piece, a small rubber wheel, and a
Christmas ornament—in various corners of the house.

He has increased by one third the chances that we will
have tandem illnesses in the month of February. Mid-
winter last year after an unrelenting siege of earaches,
throw-ups and flu, I pulled up William's pants a little fast
after an infrequent potty performance. John walked into
the bathroom in time to see the child land head first in
the toilet. "Not a bad idea," he said, "but I think he's already too big."

So where's the blessing? Well, never have we had such
a sense of camaraderie with our two older sons. The four
of us commiserate over dinner about the distress William
has brought us that day. He wrecks and loses pieces of
Lego creations, he crayons on important homework, and
with jelly hands he hugs his office-bound father good-bye.

But if he is our tormentor, he is also our court jester. He
confounds his brothers by eating all of the foods they

hate—artichokes, mushrooms, oysters, jalapeño peppers, even calf's liver, which Jack and Drew once stuffed in the waistband of their underwear to avoid eating. Regardless of the fare, he always says at least once during a meal, "Um-mmm, this such good dinner, fank you."

He works laboriously with a contraband pen and small bits of paper, then presses the scribbled scraps in his brothers' hands and says, "I make a fohnny joke for you." He waits for a lull in our conversation, then matter-of-factly throws out some non sequitur like "Jack, you know 'Come-a-Hook'?" (It took us months to recognize this garbled attempt to pronounce Incredible Hulk.) He repeats his older brothers' scatological conversations in public places. "Pee-pee in your panty hose," he yells, then slaps the side of his cheek Jack Benny style and rolls his blue eyes. He hops from his high chair after dinner and says, "Well, excuuuuuuuuuuse me."

For all of his precocious tough guy talk, he is the most tactile and often the gentlest of our boys. He moves from room to room with a cortège of stuffed animals, "Happy-dog," "Sloppy-dog," Bunny, Baby, and various down-filled blankets. He cradles a wisp of cotton in his tiny hand and says, "Sh-h-h, I got a tiny baby monkey asleep in here."

"Make a circle with hands," he yells if someone begins eating before the blessing is said. When he reaches out his small chubby hands to his brothers, it occurs to me that, though he sometimes threatens to undo us, he has united us as a family in ways we never anticipated. His silly antics, his malapropisms, his animated monologues with Teddy bears, and his childish fears all evoke stories about Jack and Drew when they were his age, shared family history about places we lived, trips we took, and people we loved that Willie won't ever know.

William's detritus for today includes a squirt gun, the nozzle for the garden hose, a tea bell, a Lego spaceman, and a plastic alligator. "Which one you want?" he asks, holding them up to me in a pilfered leftover container. "The one you don't need," I answer. He gives me the yellow alligator and goes blithely on his way distributing to his brothers and father much more than the objects in his box. Without knowing it, William has given Jack the chance to be a real big brother, the kind who loves and and protects and is proud of you, in a way he could never be with his arch rival, Drew. When Jack had the flu, William brought the filthy, much-fingered corner of his "soft cover" to his sickbed and patted Jack softly saying, "You fee' better now, Jack?" Jack didn't even say "Yuk."

William has also increased Jack's sensitivity to my frustration level. Sometimes on the verge of screaming, I am astonished to see Jack corral the rampaging little brother. "Come on, Willie, we'll go read about Froggie."

William shares Drew's room, and they are allies in the dark in elaborate imaginary games when Jack is not around. In a sense, William has given Drew a second chance at the early childhood he missed trying so hard to emulate his older brother. Of course, William has also given Drew "big brother" status and with it the irresistible power to torment a gullible younger sibling. "Know where we're going after Mom picks up the cleaning, Willie?" Drew says as we pull into a shopping center. "Yeah, we get some ice cream," William says, bouncing in his seat. "No," says Drew, grinning devilishly, "I get ice cream; Willie goes to Dr. Pharo's to get a shot."

For John, William offers absolutely unrestrained affection. The special preference that the older two have for me when they're sick or angry or sad, this coppery-haired, blue-eyed William reserves for his daddy. "Got git my daddy at the office," William says. "He not make me take a nap."

For me, he is a strange alarm clock, this sluicing sound of "soft cover" gliding over my bedroom carpet at 6 A.M. "You need a kiss," he says, smacking my elbow.

Who said three's a crowd?

Fathers and Sons

LAST SPRING Jack, Drew and William shared the chicken pox with their father. At first it was funny. Good friends brought John *Smiley's People* and coloring books. A doctor friend brought the current issue of *Playboy* with red spots carefully inked on all of the voluptuous bodies. I joked that if two more friends called to inquire about his health I could quit worrying about pallbearers. But the pox spread quickly and soon John was too sick to laugh. In twenty-four hours he looked like a teenager with a virulent case of acne; by the next morning, he resembled a victim of some medieval plague. He was home in bed for two weeks.

Neighborhood children lurked outside our quarantined house waiting to verify the rumors. "Is it true that Mr. Mackintosh has chicken pox on his gums?"

"And in his throat, ears, the underside of his eyelids and in his hair—EVERYWHERE!" I answered as I made my quick recreational dashes to the grocery store. That sufficiently fueled their imaginations so that when I returned I caught them peering in the windows of the house hoping to catch a glimpse of "Alligator Man."

Because he had no chicken pox immunity from childhood, John probably would have contracted the awful disease from his sons even if he were the most distant of fathers. Nevertheless I like to think of his pox scars as being a little like my stretch marks—visible evidence of time spent with children. And pox is fairly representative of the gratitude he often gets from these sons for his efforts.

When John and I married fourteen years ago, if I thought about children at all, I fantasized about what strong daughters he'd produce. As a Daddy's Girl myself, I thought he richly deserved the attentions that little girls tend to lavish on their fathers. He enjoys and appreciates women in a way that many Texas men don't, and he has a remarkable ability to cut through certain female affectation and small talk without being cruel or patronizing. Perhaps it's a lawyerly knack, a reluctance to accept surface appearances as sufficient evidence. He wanted daughters. I selected girls' names and packed hair ribbons each time I went to the hospital. Under his tutelage, the Mackintosh girls would have been dynamite.

But he has three sons. And his role is different, and I think harder to define. Who will he be for these boys? A patriarch? A pal? Patriarch describes none of the fathers I know. It's curious that women, regardless of their liberation, can still look lovely imitating their grand-mothers baking bread, rocking a baby or mending a ripped seam, while men imitating their grandfathers only look preposterous. Modern family life is much too casual and, at our house, too intimate for patriarchal posing.

Nor can John just be their pal. In their eyes, he is a rival for my affection. And they suspect quite correctly that he's already won. Their nightly horseplay with him often turns hostile. They know that he is the guy for whom I stuff artichokes when they'd rather have hot dogs. Once on a trip when we stopped for the night at a motel, my oldest son surveyed the bedroom with two double beds, bounced on one and announced quite innocently, "I dubs Mom," as if in alien surroundings sleeping arrangements were a toss-up.

Although I have never resorted to wait-until-your-father-gets-home tactics, these boys inevitably receive more spankings from their father than from me. The fact is, fathers who work from nine to five seldom see their children during prime time. Monday through Friday, John comes through the door about six o'clock just in time for what we call the "suicide hour." At least one son is crying, three-year-old William has dumped a bushel basket of Legos in the middle of the kitchen floor, Jack is playing "Lightly Row" on his plastic recorder relentlessly and arhythmically, someone on the phone is trying to sell me property in Pecan Plantations, and two neighbor children are posting "Ubi" (short for Ubiquitous), a scrawny stray cat, through our mail slot. Our own tomcat yowls at his empty bowl. By the time we get to the dinner table (too early for John, who needs time to unwind, and too late for starving boys who have been sneaking graham crackers since five o'clock), I feel like myelin trying desperately to flow around and cushion raw exposed nerves. William yells for ice cream as his first course, and his milk waterfalls over John's end of the table. Jack is meticulously picking the specks of pepper off his portion of salad. Drew interrupts John's courthouse war story to perform some television commercial that he thinks is hilarious. Well, it is hilarious to see this skinny, snaggle-toothed seven-year-old mimic, hawking Armourcoat Cookware. "Burnt milk, what a disaster. Might as well throw the pan away!" However, such a performance always has to be topped by his brothers, partly as a delaying tactic to avoid the coleslaw they've been pushing around their plates. The competitive uproar reaches such a pitch that somebody falls out of his chair, and John yells, "Everybody shut up and eat." "Shup your butt," William murmurs not quite under his breath. "Daddy said 'shut up,' Mom," one tattles to me as if I were deaf. William and the tattler get popped for their impudence, and a somewhat strained order is restored.

They never miss an opportunity to point out their father's shortcomings to me. Because he's willing to scramble on the floor with them and sometimes eats potato chips before supper, they figure he's one of them and should be subject to the same corrective scrutiny. I once remarked at the dinner table, after a headache-inducing, smoke-filled session with an old friend, that if I'd married a man who smoked I'd probably have thrown him out by now. "Daddy smokes!" they chorused hopefully. (He smokes approximately one cigar a week while mowing the yard.)

I try to see him through their eyes. "Dads are just bodyguards for Moms," Jack grumbles. "They do all the rough stuff." He hugs and squeezes them daily, but they squirm to get away. He was the one who placed transatlantic calls to them while we were in London in the spring. They know they're loved, but they also know that their father does not hang on their every word when he's at home. I sometimes envy his ability to tune them out. How many times must I hear a complete recounting of *The Empire Strikes Back?*

And sometimes they tune him out. About once a month, he asks them if they'd like to see his stamp collection. Their eyes glaze over and they sigh as he recites the benefits of stamp collecting. He gets the huge volumes down from his closet and insists that they look at the passion of his boyhood. Breathes there a man of my generation who did not send off for some Mozambique triangles?

They listen intently to his stories about his stint in the Army, and Jack, who is contemplating six-man football next year, was particularly relieved to hear his dad say that he was scared to death the first time he put on pads and helmet. However, his legal profession is hardly the sort of job that fires the imagination of small boys. When Jack and Drew were much younger, they were especially awestruck by the carpenters and painters who came to our house with tool boxes and ladders. When these heroes finished for the day and drove away, one of the boys would look wistfully after them and say, "I wonder when Daddy is going to get his pickup truck." Their father's deficiency in the manual arts was further confirmed in the Father-Son Derby Day held at the local YMCA. The racing car that John and Jack labored over all weekend veered off the track just inches from the starting line while the boys with engineers for fathers, who had skillfully weighted the front ends of their cars, cheered their sleek models to victory. Jack's car won an award for looking the most like a seven-year-old had built it. "We got the wrong kind of Daddy," Jack said, slamming the door to his room.

But they're older now, and they listen with at least one ear when John tries to explain just what it is that he does all day. His influence is apparent when they plot revenge on a neighborhood bully. "Let's sue him!" I also hope I remembered to tell John about the bulletin board in Drew's first-grade classroom. The teacher had written, "I wish I could be a grown-up so I could . . ." The children had drawn fanciful pictures illustrating such adult pleasures as "so I could eat all the ice cream I want before supper," or "so I could watch Saturday Night Live." It took me a minute to find Drew's picture on the board. He had drawn a drab stick figure man dressed in a black suit with a large brown square hooked on his left hand. The caption, "So I could settle cases."

Sometimes they even respond sympathetically to his reports of frustration or defeat at the courthouse. "Dad, is it sort of like when we're setting up the army men in our sandpile and it's real hot and the sand flies keep getting in your face and the sweat keeps stinging your eyes and your men fall down?" "Yeah, sort of like that." "Well, Daddy, don't they ever let you use a pencil when you do your work so you can erase if you make a mistake?"

They see him when he's tired, when he's preoccupied, and they know that many of the fishing trips he promises out of guilt on Wednesday may not materialize on Saturday. But if I ask them which parent has the most fun, they would, without hesitation, say, "Daddy does." Fathers don't relinquish the pleasures of their childhoods the way most mothers seem to do. Or perhaps it's just that the pleasures of female childhood were often hours spent pretending we were grown-ups. I see plenty of fathers shooting a few baskets on the school playground, but no mothers skipping rope or playing jacks. John emerges soaked from supervising three boys in the bathtub. "Boy, they really had a good time in there tonight. We lined the army men up on the rim of the tub and shot 'em with the water guns." Who had a good time? They know that their father will be a kid with them when it comes to playing pinball machines, shooting fireworks on the Fourth of July, or yelling at the Dallas Cowboys.

Remembering his own childhood with a retired grandfather, John worries that his sons are not fishing enough. Will they have no stories to tell their children about bullfrogs getting caught on trot lines? Will they never know the pleasures of seining up minnows? He takes the older two on camping weekends, and they return with conflicting reports. They loved it/hated it. Trips alone with their father always have an element of risk that both attracts and repels these sons. They know in advance that the number of soda pops consumed will not be closely monitored. John may let them "drive" the car or, even better, the boat. On the other hand, if their fishing lines get tangled in the cattails or if they hook their own sock, they may just have to "tough it out." Daddies do not martyr themselves on vacations. On one particular trip, John and his good friend Walter got the poor little urchins out of bed in the middle of the night for a snipe hunt. We have pictures of the children intently holding their pillowcase traps with expressions of stark horror on their faces. Needless to say, the little boys sulked all the way home, and the dads got no thanks for the weekend, but as Walter said, "You never forget the guy who takes you on your first snipe hunt."

Because John is not with these boys day in and day out, he can't know their emotional and physical limits as well as I do. I know what offends them, what sends them to their rooms in tears and also what is likely to heal their ill tempers. Once when Drew felt so put upon by his older and younger brothers that he was threatening to leave home, I told him about the time I packed to run away when I was five. "You know what I put in the suitcase?" "What?" he asked, wiping his nose and his tears on his shirtsleeve. "Five pairs of panties and a package of Fig Newtons." The frown he tried so desperately to maintain finally gave way. "Mom, you were so dumb," he said, shaking his head as he returned to the fracas. Now, when I hear the fierce slamming of his door upstairs, I just yell, "Hey, you pack the panties; I've got the Fig Newtons." It usually gets the door open again.

I know them *too* well. Without the scrutiny of the real world that their father innocently brings from time to time, they'd probably never grow up. John looks at Drew's art masterpiece from kindergarten and says, "Hey, man, how come your cat has seven legs?" Mothers have been schooled to say only, "Tell me about your picture, dear." My boys know where to go for an honest appraisal of their abilities. I let them win at card games; John never does.

They also respect him as the custodian of certain male knowledge that will stand them in good stead with their peers. With him, they have learned to rig their own fishing lines, to throw and catch a baseball competently and to speak knowledgeably of people with names like "Too Tall" Jones, Yastremzki, and Pelé.

He understands and shares their need for physical workouts. He hardly gets his tie off in the afternoon before they have him running football plays with them in the front yard. He runs at the track with them, shoots baskets with them and doesn't try very hard to mask his enthusiasm for their athletic prowess.

Neither one of us would be a sufficient parent alone. Not only do we need the comfort of our conspiratorial crossed eyes or winks above their eye level that say, "They're here temporarily; we're here for the long haul, baby"; we also realize that our individual aspirations and concerns for these sons need balancing. If he pushes them too hard physically, so hard that somebody comes in from the front yard hiccuping, "I hate Daddy. I'm never gonna' play with him again," then I admit that I get too pushy about the music lessons and the books they haven't read. If they express enthusiasm for playing the recorder in music class at school, I have a neighbor's borrowed flute waiting for them when they get home the next afternoon. If they applaud Shakespeare in the band shell at Fair Park, I check out everything the children's section of the library has to offer on the Renaissance.

John worries too much about their bodies. Perhaps it's just from his years of supervising their baths. He daily notes the progress of their ripply permanent teeth, the healing of their scabs and the collapse of their arches. He once brought William to me after his bath and said, "I really think this child ought to see the pediatrician. This mole on his collarbone is new. It's a funny color and shape. I think it ought to be removed." Flicking the greenish speck with my fingernail, I grinned triumphantly, "And you are the only father I know who would have us biopsy a booger."

If I temper his concern for their physical well-being, he similarly assures me that their passion for pinball machines is not a definitive indication of their intelligence. I'm not so sure. I did a lot of ridiculous pretending when I was a kid. Some days I was Sheena, Queen of the Jungle, with leopards for escorts. Other days I dramatically conducted radio symphonies in front of the mirror. Still, I'm not prepared for sons who walk around pulling imaginary levers and saying, "P'ding, ching-ching-ching, wong, wong, ching-ching-ching."

He sometimes reads to them at night or agrees to tell them a story. I sometimes recognize his made-up story as the thinly disguised plot of *The Bourne Identity*, which he just put down. We both tuck them in, but I am the greater sucker for their delaying tactics, drinks of water and philosophical questions like, "Why does God let people get trampled at rock concerts?" I once read most of the Book of Job to Jack at 9 P.M. John predicts he'll request *War and Peace* tomorrow night.

Fourteen years ago, I was in love with his prematurely gray hair, his ability to quote Shakespeare and his brilliant analysis of Adlai Stevenson's political career. Now I'm just glad that he can get his boys in bed in fifteen seconds flat.

CHRISTIAN HERALD ASSOCIATION AND ITS MINISTRIES

CHRISTIAN HERALD ASSOCIATION, founded in 1878, publishes The Christian Herald Magazine, one of the leading interdenominational religious monthlies in America. Through its wide circulation, it brings inspiring articles and the latest news of religious developments to many families. From the magazine's pages came the initiative for CHRISTIAN HERALD CHILDREN'S HOME and THE BOWERY MISSION, two individually supported not-for-profit corporations.

CHRISTIAN HERALD CHILDREN'S HOME, established in 1894, is the name for a unique and dynamic ministry to disadvantaged children, offering hope and opportunities which would not otherwise be available for reasons of poverty and neglect. The goal is to develop each child's potential and to demonstrate Christian compassion and understanding to children in need.

Mont Lawn is a permanent camp located in Bushkill, Pennsylvania. It is the focal point of a ministry which provides a healthful "vacation with a purpose" to children who without it would be confined to the streets of the city. Up to 1000 children between the ages of 7 and 11 come to Mont Lawn each year.

Christian Herald Children's Home maintains year-round contact with children by means of an *In-City Youth Ministry*. Central to its philosophy is the belief that only through sustained relationships and demonstrated concern can individual lives be truly enriched. Special emphasis is on individual guidance, spiritual and family counseling and tutoring. This follow-up ministry to inner-city children culminates for many in financial assistance toward higher education and career counseling.

THE BOWERY MISSION, located at 227 Bowery, New York City, has since 1879 been reaching out to the lost men on the Bowery, offering them what could be their last chance to rebuild their lives. Every man is fed, clothed and ministered to. Countless numbers have entered the 90-day residential rehabilitation program at the Bowery Mission. A concentrated ministry of counseling, medical care, nutrition therapy, Bible study and Gospel services awakens a man to spiritual renewal within himself.

These ministries are supported solely by the voluntary contributions of individuals and by legacies and bequests. Contributions are tax deductible. Checks should be made out either to CHRISTIAN HERALD CHILDREN'S HOME or to THE BOWERY MISSION.

Administrative Office: 40 Overlook Drive, Chappaqua, New York 10514
Telephone: (914) 769-9000